Commendations for A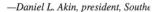

"My friend and colleague Scott
his book *Answering God's Call*. .
practically helpful. It will be a b.
know, obey, and fulfill his calling

—*Daniel L. Akin, president, Southe*

"One of the most enduring, and at times perplexing, questions Christians wrestle with
has to do with God's 'call' on our individual lives. *Answering God's Call* is an essential contribution to the Hobbs College Library. This resource meets each individual
at the intersection of future-tense thinking and God's desired will. Dr. Pace serves as
both author and architect allowing the reader to clarify and then construct a life rich
with calling that is firmly grounded in a doctrine of vocation."

—*Brent Crowe, vice president, Student Leadership University*

"*Answering God's Call* provides a great biblical guide for church leaders to disciple
a new generation of leaders for God's mission in their community and around the
world. I highly recommend the book and urge pastors to make it an integral part of
their leadership development process."

—*Kevin Ezell, president, North American Mission Board*

"Increasingly, people are realizing that the question 'What should I do with my life?'
is a needless and wearisome burden. The better question is, 'What is God calling
me to do with the gifts, talents, and passions that he has given to me?' *Answering God's Call* is accessible, insightful, and encouraging as it recovers the classic
Christian understanding of calling, removing the all-too-common burden of choice
and replacing it with the easy yoke of serving God and serving others."

—*Gene C. Fant Jr., president, North Greenville University*

"The question of God's call is among the more regular questions I receive as a pastor.
Too often people seem to ground their understanding of God's call in emotion, almost
exclusively. That's why I love and appreciate this volume from Scott Pace. It tackles
the question of God's call from both a biblical and pastoral perspective. You will be
helped by this book."

—*Micah Fries, senior pastor, Brainerd Baptist Church, Chattanooga, TN*

"A scholarly and approachable book on a vitally important question: How do we
know what God's will is for our lives? Dr. Pace answers the question biblically
and practically in a way that avoids the extremes that often stymie this discussion.
Whether you are trying to figure out God's call on your life or how to help others
discover it, you will want to own and master this book!"

—*J. D. Greear, pastor, The Summit Church, Raleigh-Durham, NC, and president,*
   The Southern Baptist Convention

"What I would have given to have had this series when I first came to faith in Christ. To me, understanding my calling has been my staying power in ministry. Next to my call, my spiritual growth as a believer has grounded me for the duration of my life and ministry. Read and be enriched."

—Johnny Hunt, senior vice president of evangelism and leadership, North American Mission Board; pastor, First Baptist Church, Woodstock, GA; and former president, The Southern Baptist Convention

"*Answering God's Call* is a brilliant work delivered at a significant moment in history. This generation is intensely curious about finding purpose and meaning for their lives. The great news found in God's Word is that the Lord calls his people to particular ministries and profound opportunities for impact that correspond exactly to the way he creates each of us. Pace draws clear lines from the biblical foundations for discerning calling to very practical means for investigating God's leading. This work is a gift to those seeking to find the joy of work God has laid out before them and the means for enduring in joy in that calling."

—Kevin Peck, lead pastor, The Austin Stone Community Church, Austin, TX

"God is at work all over the world redeeming a people to himself, and every Jesus follower is called to share in this mission. I'm so thankful for Scott Pace's new book, *Answering God's Call*, that encourages every believer to discover their God-called place in this glorious task. His practical insights and biblical guidance will help every Jesus follower discover God's unique call on their life and then fulfill it by leveraging their life for the sake of God's eternal mission."

—Vance Pitman, senior pastor, Hope Church, Las Vegas, NV

"In a day when many young people are walking away from religion, God is still calling men and women to serve him in vocational ministry or through their career platforms. This resource will help you discern God's call on your life and develop a path forward in pursuit of that call. What a gift to churches, pastors, and those who mentor young leaders!"

—Jimmy Scroggins, lead pastor, Family Church, West Palm Beach, FL

Commendations for Hobbs College Library

"This series honors a wonderful servant of Christ with a stellar lineup of contributors. What a gift to the body of Christ! My hope and prayer is that it will be widely read and used for the glory of God and the good of his Church."

—*Daniel L. Akin, president, Southeastern Baptist Theological Seminary*

"This series is a must have, go-to resource for everyone who is serious about Bible study, teaching, and preaching. The authors are committed to the authority of the Bible and the vitality of the local church. I am excited about the kingdom impact of this much needed resource."

—*Hance Dilbeck, executive director, Baptist General Convention of Oklahoma*

"I am very excited about the dynamic leadership of Dr. Heath Thomas and his vision of the Hobbs College Library at Oklahoma Baptist University that he is developing. Through his work as Dean of the Hobbs College of Theology, this 21-volume set of books will ascend the theological understanding of laypeople, church leaders, pastors, and bi-vocational pastors. Therefore, I want to encourage you to participate in this vision that will equip your church to make a greater difference for Jesus Christ in your community and around the world."

—*Ronnie Floyd, president, the Southern Baptist Convention Executive Committee*

"This series offers an outstanding opportunity for leaders of all kind to strengthen their knowledge of God, his word, and the manner in which we should engage the culture around us. Do not miss this opportunity to grow as a disciple of Jesus and as a leader of his church."

—*Micah Fries, senior pastor, Brainerd Baptist Church, Chattanooga, TN*

"The Hobbs College Library is a perfect way to help people who want to grow in the basics of their faith. Whether you are a layperson or longtime pastor, this tool will help give you the theological base needed for ministry today. I highly recommend this tremendous resource to anyone wanting to deepen their understanding of Scripture."

—*Jack Graham, pastor, Prestonwood Baptist Church, North TX, and former president, the Southern Baptist Convention*

"The best resources are those that develop the church theologically while instructing her practically in the work of the Great Commission. Dr. Thomas has assembled an impressive host of contributors for a new set of resources that will equip leaders at all levels who want to leave a lasting impact for the gospel. Dr. Hobbs exemplified the pastor-leader-theologian, and it's inspiring to see a series put out in his name that so aptly embodies his ministry and calling."

—*J.D. Greear, pastor, The Summit Church, Raleigh-Durham, NC, and president, the Southern Baptist Convention*

ANSWERING GOD'S CALL

HOBBS COLLEGE LIBRARY

ANSWERING GOD'S CALL

Finding, Following and Fulfilling
God's Will for Your Life

R. SCOTT PACE

HEATH A. THOMAS, *Editor*

OBU

ACADEMIC

NASHVILLE, TENNESSEE

∞∞

Dedicated to

Gracelyn, Tyler, Tessa, and Cassie,

For the greatest joy as your father,

That you may walk in the truth

As you answer God's call

∞∞

Contents

Acknowledgments

I was raised in a Christian home by parents who faithfully served the Lord in their marketplace professions. They modeled what it looked like to make a difference for Christ in the workplace. My intention when I chose an educational path was to follow in their steps. I selected a school based on the career path I thought would ultimately provide the life I envisioned for my future family. After graduating with an accounting degree and working in the public and private sectors for a few years, God steered my heart in a different direction. Through my personal walk with Christ and my active involvement in the local church, I learned how to discern God's will for my life, and I surrendered to his calling.

Although I never could have imagined the plans he had for me, much of what I learned along the way from Scripture and from those who invested in my journey helped me to understand a pathway to hearing God's voice and following his call. In many ways, this book is the culmination of those experiences and the blueprint for how I continue to navigate God's will today. I have had the privilege of sharing them with others in a variety of ministry contexts over the years who find themselves wandering through life and wondering what God's plan is for them. My prayer is that the Lord will continue to use these biblical truths to help others find, follow, and fulfill his will for their lives.

I'm thankful to my friend and colleague, Heath Thomas, for the opportunity to contribute another volume to the Hobbs College Library. Your vision to produce a unique series of books that blend academic substance with practical guidance for the purpose of personal development and ministry service has inspired me. I'm grateful for your passion for Christ, his church, and for your investment in others who desire to serve him faithfully. It's always a joy to partner together, especially with B&H Academic, whose team continues to amaze me with its dedication to excellence, its personal support for authors and their ideas, and its commitment to producing content to further God's kingdom.

In fulfilling God's call on my life, I have been blessed to serve several churches, Oklahoma Baptist University, and other ministry partners that have contributed to my own formation and understanding of calling. I now have the privilege of teaching at Southeastern Baptist Theological Seminary, serving as the dean of The College at Southeastern, and investing in students who desire to leverage their lives for the cause of Christ. I'm eternally grateful for the support of the SEBTS faculty and family, especially President Akin, who not only inspire me to grow personally and professionally, but also give me every opportunity to do so.

Of course, words cannot express my gratitude for my wife, Dana, whom God providentially and graciously gifted to me as part of his will for my life. Her love and support have helped me answer God's call and navigate his plan, and her tireless effort to care for our family models for them the love of Christ and how to serve our Savior faithfully. I'm grateful for Gracelyn, Tyler, Tessa, and Cassie and pray that the truths in this book would be useful in guiding them into a deeper love for Jesus and an unconditional surrender to his will for their lives.

To my beloved Savior and exalted King, Jesus Christ, may you receive the honor and glory for any fruit born by this labor of love given as an offering to you!

About the Library

The Hobbs College Library equips Christians with tools for growing in the faith and for effective ministry. The library trains its readers in three major areas: Bible, theology, and ministry. The series originates from the Herschel H. Hobbs College of Theology and Ministry at Oklahoma Baptist University, where biblical, orthodox, and practical education lies at its core. Training the next generation was important for the great Baptist statesman Dr. Herschel H. Hobbs, and the Hobbs College that bears his name fosters that same vision.

The Hobbs College Library: Biblical. Orthodox. Practical.

PART I

ANSWERING GOD'S CALL

We all know what it's like. Our phone rings, and an unrecognized number appears on the screen. Immediately we try to discern, *who* is calling me? and why are they calling *me*? Before we're willing to commit to a conversation, we want to know the identity of the one trying to reach us. Their identity can help us to determine why they are calling and, specifically, what it has to do with us. Oftentimes, when we can't immediately verify the source of the call, we ignore it. We send it to voicemail. We think, "If it's important, they'll call back."

But God's call on one's life is not like this everyday experience. When the Creator of the universe calls, we can't ignore it, delay our response by sending it to spiritual voicemail, or dismiss it as a wrong number as though God mistakenly called us. We must answer him. But the same questions that influence whether or not we answer our phone also determine how we respond to God's call. *Who* is calling you, and why the caller is specifically calling *you,* both have implications that impact every area of your life. Therefore, it is crucial for us to explore how the Lord calls an individual, why he calls people to specific tasks, and how we can discern his personal will for our lives as we answer his call.

Our Universal Calling as Christians

The whole concept of "calling" is often approached with a mystical understanding. Many people assume that when someone refers to "being called," it is referring exclusively to vocational ministry. But this ignores or overlooks the fact that as believers we all have a calling on our lives. This fundamental understanding of God's calling is repeatedly affirmed throughout Scripture and involves three primary aspects.

First, *the Christian calling is a call to salvation*. Scripture describes salvation as the foundational aspect of our calling, as we "were called by [God] into fellowship with his Son, Jesus Christ our Lord" (1 Cor 1:9). This is why the Bible identifies all believers as "those who are the called" (Jude 1:1) and as those who "share in a heavenly calling" (Heb 3:1). The Scriptures also speak of salvation in terms of the "eternal life" to which we "were called" (1 Tim 6:12), as the inheritance from the One "who calls [us] into his own kingdom and glory" (1 Thess 2:12), and that which we pursue as the prize of "God's heavenly call in Christ Jesus" (Phil 3:14).

The call to salvation is universally extended through the grace of God (Titus 2:11), but it must be personally received through faith in Jesus Christ (Eph 2:8). When we receive Christ as Lord and Savior, we are responding to God's call. The reality of our salvation is the truth that enlightens the eyes of our hearts to "know what is the hope of his calling, what is the wealth of his glorious inheritance in the saints" (Eph 1:18).

In addition to our salvation, *the Christian calling is a call to serve*. This means that it is not only a heavenly calling, but also a humble calling. Jesus taught us that he "did not come to be served, but to serve, and to give his life as a ransom for many" (Matt 20:28). Our Lord demonstrated a genuine heart to serve as he washed his disciples' feet on the night before he would pay the ultimate sacrifice for them on the cross (John 13:4–14). As he concluded this display of humble service, he instructed them, "For I have given you an example, that you also should do just as I have done for you" (v. 15).

When Jesus invites us to follow him, it is not simply a decision to receive eternal life and forgiveness for our sins. He invites us to learn from him, specifically his humility of heart (Matt 11:28–29), so that we might embrace his same disposition. But the calling to serve is not merely an attitude of service; it must be lived out in acts of service. God calls us to "serve one another through love" (Gal 5:13) with an attitude that reflects the heart of Jesus, considering others as more important than ourselves, not looking out for our own interests, but for the interests of others (Phil 2:3–5).

The third truth we must recognize is that *the Christian calling is a call to surrender*. Our salvation was purchased by the "precious blood of Christ" (1 Pet 1:18–19). His payment for our sins identifies us as his disciples whose lives belong to him (1 Cor 6:19–20). This means that as we receive eternal life from him we simultaneously surrender our lives to him (Matt 16:24–27). We submit to him as our Lord, the King of our hearts, and Ruler over our lives (2 Cor 5:15). Therefore, we are called to offer our lives continually as living sacrifices (Rom 12:1), fully surrendered to honoring him by fulfilling his mission (Matt 28:18–20).

Giving God control of our lives is an ongoing act of moment-by-moment submission to him. It involves everything from life-altering decisions to life's everyday decisions. In all things, you are called to "live worthy of the calling you have received" (Eph 4:1). This means that our lives must be set apart for his purposes, for

3

"he has saved us and called us with a holy calling" (2 Tim 1:9; cf. 1 Thess 4:7; 1 Pet 1:15–16). While there will be times that we fall short and temporarily reassume control of our lives, God's loving discipline will lead us to a renewed heart of surrender and submission to him.

God's calling for all believers is a heavenly calling, a humble calling, and a holy calling. When we trust Christ we are embracing his call to salvation, his call to serve, and his call to surrender. In this sense, we are all called!

Our Unique Calling as Christians

The universal nature of God's calling for all believers does not eliminate his personalized calling. We share the fundamental elements of our calling, but there are unique aspects as well. The Lord has chosen *you* to serve him in a particular way, at a specific place and time, with a unique combination of talents and gifts, for his strategic purpose.

God Desires to Use You. Throughout history, God has graciously chosen to work through the lives of his people to accomplish his plan. His use of particular individuals for strategic and specific purposes demonstrates his desire to use each of us. God specifically called Noah to build the ark (Genesis 6), selected Abraham to be the father of the nations (Genesis 12), and chose Moses to deliver his people (Exod 3). He also called Samuel to be his prophet (1 Samuel 3), David to be his king (1 Samuel 16), and Solomon to build his temple (2 Samuel 7; cf. 1 Kings 5). Esther was chosen as God's instrument at a particular time and place (Esth 4:14). Isaiah and Jeremiah also had specific callings as God's spokesmen (Isa 6:1–8; Jer 1:5). Similarly, Jesus personally selected his apostles (John 15:16), including Paul (Gal 1:15–16; cf. 1 Cor 15:8), with a specific plan for their lives.

In the same way, God has designed you to serve in a unique role within his master plan. He saved you with a specific purpose in mind. God is calling you, just as Paul instructed Timothy, to "fulfill *your* ministry" (2 Tim 4:5). Similar to his message to Archippus, you must, "Pay attention to the ministry you have received in the Lord, so that you can accomplish it" (Col 4:17). For some this involves serving God in a vocational capacity as a minister or a missionary. Although there certainly are distinct calls to serve the Lord in this way, your specific calling may not be to a formal ministry or foreign mission field. But this does not minimize your calling as though it is less significant. The proper understanding of your vocation is to embrace your career as your calling. In fact, the term *vocation* literally means "calling"! God uses all kinds of professional fields of service as part of his kingdom here on earth. God has gifted you and prepared you for a unique calling that he has for your life!

God Is Determined to Use You. When you consider the people in the Bible that God chose, we often think of them as iconic heroes. But we must be careful to recognize that God did not use them because they were exceptional; he used them because they were available. The patriarchs were all flawed people just like us. Abraham lied to people and laughed at the absurdity of God's plan. David sinned miserably. Jonah fled fearfully. Peter denied Christ repeatedly. Yet God was able to use them.

God wants you to "consider your calling" in the same way that Paul challenged the Corinthian believers (1 Cor 1:26–28). It is not in spite of our weaknesses that God has called us; it is because of them! By accomplishing great things through modest people, the Lord's greatness is magnified. Therefore, we do not have to fear that God cannot use us, or that he is unwilling to use us. In fact, we don't even have to pray for God to use us! He has promised that he will use us. We simply have to be "usable." As you seek to fulfill God's calling by devoting yourself to holiness, you will become "a special instrument, set apart, useful to the Master, prepared for every good work" (2 Tim 2:21).

Looking Ahead

God is calling you and you must answer the call. He has called you as his child and as Christ's disciple to serve him with a submissive and surrendered heart. He is also calling you for a specific and strategic purpose that he wants to accomplish through you. The chapters in this section will help you to confirm and clarify God's specific call on your life. As you discern his plan for you, we will also explore practical steps you can begin to take as you answer his call.

CHAPTER 1

Confirming God's Call on Your Life

When I began serving in ministry, a church member invited me to join him for a business trip. As an accountant who was going to perform an audit, he thought he could use some help. Since I had graduated from college with a degree in accounting and had worked in the field before surrendering to the ministry, he asked me if I'd like to come. As a young youth pastor, newly married, and still in seminary, any extra income was a blessing. So I agreed.

My friend was successful. He had a loving family, a beautiful home, a comfortable life, and he loved the Lord. One night as we took a break for supper, he admitted that as a younger man he had felt called to ministry. Based on his current life situation, I assumed he had concluded that his ministry would be in the field of accounting. After all, God's calling is not limited to vocational ministry; he uses all types of careers for his kingdom purposes. But as he explained that evening, he had taken a step back from ministry to work as an accountant and had never returned to his true calling. When I probed further, he confessed that it would be "impossible" for him at this stage to abandon his career, alter his lifestyle, and pursue vocational ministry. It was too late, he said. He had resigned himself to living with the knowledge that he had abandoned his calling.

The sad reality is that many believers fall into this same category. Some decisions to walk away are intentional, as believers count the cost and are unwilling to make the necessary sacrifices to follow God's will for their lives. But the cost and sacrifice of not obeying Christ is far greater. They are haunted by regret and are left to wonder "what if?" for the rest of their lives. Others don't intentionally disobey God; they simply never discern their calling and end up pursuing what seems most natural, enjoyable, or comfortable. They often live with an undiscerned void and never quite identify the source of their discontent.

The disappointing truth of a Christian failing to fulfill God's plan as a result of ignorance or disobedience is tragic and far too common. But the Scriptures provide us the counsel we need to confirm our calling. In Paul's letter to the Galatians, he defended his calling in order to validate the message of the gospel and his ministry. His description of his personal experience provides for us a deeper understanding of the nature of God's calling and how it can be confirmed.

Galatians 1:11–24: [11]For I want you to know, brothers and sisters, that the gospel preached by me is not of human origin. [12]For I did not receive it from a human source and I was not taught it, but it came by a revelation of Jesus Christ.

[13]For you have heard about my former way of life in Judaism: I intensely persecuted God's church and tried to destroy it. [14]I advanced in Judaism beyond many contemporaries among my people, because I was extremely zealous for the traditions of my ancestors. [15]But when God, who from my mother's womb set me apart and called me by his grace, was pleased [16]to reveal his Son in me, so that I could preach him among the Gentiles, I did not immediately consult with anyone. [17]I did not go up to Jerusalem to

those who had become apostles before me; instead I went to Arabia and came back to Damascus.

[18]Then after three years I did go up to Jerusalem to get to know Cephas, and I stayed with him fifteen days. [19]But I didn't see any of the other apostles except James, the Lord's brother. [20]I declare in the sight of God: I am not lying in what I write to you.

[21]Afterward, I went to the regions of Syria and Cilicia. [22]I remained personally unknown to the Judean churches that are in Christ. [23]They simply kept hearing: "He who formerly persecuted us now preaches the faith he once tried to destroy." [24]And they glorified God because of me.

Your Calling Must Be Authentic

Whenever we hear unbelievable news about a friend or read a startling report on social media, our immediate response is typically, is this true?! Our willingness to accept the reliability of the information largely depends on the credibility of the source. If we know the person we heard it from or can verify that the source is valid, then we will respond accordingly. However, if the source is one that is unfamiliar or unreliable, we are likely to dismiss the information.

Similarly, the first aspect of confirming God's call on your life must be to verify the source. Is your calling authentic? The false teachers that were deceiving the Galatians were attempting to discredit Paul. If they could undermine his credibility, they would be able to discount his message and his ministry. Paul defended the authenticity of his calling in order to validate the unbelievable good news of the gospel. His defense of his ministry provides us with a model of how our own calling can be authenticated.

Paul's experience teaches us that *a genuine calling is received from Christ*. While traveling on the road to Damascus to secure warrants for the persecution of Christians, Paul was confronted by a glorious appearance of Christ (Acts 9:1–5). In this encounter, he was converted and would subsequently receive his calling. The Lord said, "This man is my chosen instrument to take my name to Gentiles, kings, and Israelites" (v. 15). To authenticate his message and his ministry, he specifically told the Galatians that the gospel he preached was not received from an unreliable or secondary source, but from Jesus Christ himself (Gal 1:11–12).

Although Jesus may not physically appear to you in a "Damascus road" experience, your calling must be received from him. This means that your calling will be spiritually discerned within the context of your own personal relationship with Christ. To receive his calling, we must first be confronted with our sinfulness and converted by saving faith in Christ as our sacrificial substitute. Through his death, burial, and resurrection, we can be forgiven for our sin, rescued from his judgment, and redeemed for his glory. His payment for our sin restores our relationship with God, adopts us into his family, and enlists us in his mission.

As we grow in our relationship with Jesus, he will reveal his specific calling for our lives. But we must be careful to discern the nature of that calling. Oftentimes Christians who sincerely desire to serve the Lord, who are compelled by grace and gratitude, and who want to make a difference for Christ can surrender to a "calling" that seems to be more spiritual or more significant. Sometimes believers embrace a perceived calling that is imposed on them by well-meaning parents, friends, or spiritual leaders. Others who genuinely want what is best for us can pressure us into making decisions. They have good intentions, but they may not be God's intentions. Although both of these scenarios can sometimes be part of what

God uses to call us, the ultimate authority for our calling comes from Christ.

The apostle's testimony also teaches us that *a genuine calling results in change*. Galatians 1 describes the radical change that resulted from his calling. He recounts his "former way of life" that was characterized by his persecution of the church in his zeal for his religious heritage (vv. 13–14). But God's call changed everything. To speak of it as his "former" way of life not only describes it as a previous lifestyle, but it also indicates that his new life is definitively and dramatically different. He went from punishing the cause of Christ to promoting the cause of Christ!

God's calling on our lives should also produce a drastic change. For those who previously indulged in blatant and rebellious sin, conversion will produce a transformation that will be obvious. For others who lived a moral lifestyle, salvation may not significantly alter their social behavior or personal demeanor. However, the change that Christ makes when you receive your calling always results in a significant change of direction. The trajectory of your life—its purpose, its motivation, its path, and its destination—is substantially altered. These fundamental aspects of your life are completely redefined by your calling.

As with the apostle Paul, our calling must be authenticated. We must discern God's call on our lives through our personal relationship with Christ. We must listen for and recognize the voice of our Shepherd and distinguish his calling from other voices (John 10:4–5). As we authenticate our calling from him, we should recognize the shift in direction of our lives. Our passions and pursuits will begin to flow from our calling and saturate our lives with a desire to fulfill it.

Your Calling Must Have Authority

When our calling is authenticated as coming from the Lord, it automatically means that it should have authority over our lives. But, as Paul goes on to describe his calling, he reveals in greater detail the definitive nature of its authority and the practical implications.

God's will for our lives has authority because *our calling is a divine plan*. Paul states that God "set [him] apart" for his plan before he was born (v. 15). This mirrors Jeremiah's description of God's calling on his life, "I chose you before I formed you in the womb; I set you apart before you were born. I appointed you a prophet to the nations" (Jer 1:5). In his providence, God, who works all things according to the purpose of his will (Eph 1:11), also has a divine plan for each of us. The One who knit you together in your mother's womb foresees each one of your days before you ever live the first one (Ps 139:13, 16)! His divine calling on our life possesses an inherent authority that deserves and demands our submission to it.

As we surrender to his plan, we are also assured that *our calling is accomplished by divine power*. Paul indicates that God set him apart for this calling "by his grace" (Gal 1:15). He recognized that the compelling nature of God's calling does not obligate us against our wills, but his grace enables and empowers us to fulfill it. Paul cooperated with God's divine strength to accomplish everything God called him to do. He reflected, "By the grace of God I am what I am, and his grace toward me was not in vain. On the contrary, I worked harder than any of them, yet not I, but the grace of God that was with me" (1 Cor 15:10).

In Christ, God graciously provides everything you need to accomplish his calling on your life (2 Pet 1:3; cf. Phil 4:13). But apart from him, you will not be able to fulfill his plan (John 15:5). This means that if you devote yourself to something you can accomplish in your own strength, according to your own wisdom, and with your own ability, then you are achieving something less than God's will. His calling on your life will require his divine power. But, by his grace, he can accomplish "above and beyond all that we ask or think according to the power that works in us" (Eph 3:20).

In addition to these truths, Paul's testimony also teaches that *our calling accomplishes a divine purpose*. God had a specific goal for Paul's life, for him to "preach [Christ] among the Gentiles" (v. 16). The nature of God's calling on our lives is decisively spiritual. We often view our calling through an earthly lens that finds meaning and value in what we achieve or acquire. But the authority of his call on our lives derives from the eternal purpose for which the Lord desires to use us.

God's will for you is a privileged opportunity. He has invited you to be an integral part of his eternal plan. No matter what specific role you play, his call on your life is part of redemptive history and a plan that is larger than any one individual or group of people. He desires to use you in a strategic and significant way to reach the nations for Christ. And your willingness and availability to serve according to your unique role will be used by God to accomplish his divine purpose.

But God's calling on our lives will only be as effective as our submission to its authority. On September 2, 1945, Japan, as the final nation of the Axis powers, effectively ended World War II when it signed a declaration that conceded defeat to the allies. In summation, the document stated, "We hereby surrender all forces under our control." This official pronouncement is historically known as the Instrument of Unconditional Surrender. In the same way, spiritually speaking, we must surrender control of all areas of our lives to him. His calling must have authority.

This means that our personal ambitions, desires, and life goals must be surrendered to God's calling on our lives. Although our calling may not always require us to abandon everything, its authority means that we must be willing to do so. God asked Abraham to leave his country and his extended family (Gen 12:1). God asked him to trust him for a miracle (Gen 17:15–21). He even asked him to sacrifice his son in faith and obedience (Gen 22:2). By faith, Abraham surrendered himself to God's plan (Heb 11:8–12, 17–19). Similarly, God will lead us to surrender everything to him until our submission to his calling is complete.

Although this submission will be difficult, it also will provide us with hope. There will be days in your ministry that you will feel lost and lonely. You will experience defeat and disappointment, and you will walk through seasons of hurt and heartache. In those times, you will be tempted to explore other possibilities and will seriously consider walking away. But your calling will be the anchor that does not allow you to drift in the storms of doubt and despair. You won't give up, because you know you can't. You've been called. At times your calling will be all that you can cling to, all that you have to keep you going. But, be reassured, "He who calls you is faithful" (1 Thess 5:24). The good work that he has begun in you, he will continue it until his plan for you is ultimately fulfilled in Christ Jesus (Phil 1:6). For we know, the eyes of the Lord are surveying the earth, looking to support "those who are wholeheartedly devoted to him" (2 Chr 16:9).

Your Calling Must Be Affirmed

The final aspect of confirming your call is the affirmation process that cements it. Verifying God's calling involves three critical steps that are reflected in Paul's experience (Gal 1:16–24). Paul's calling was verified first through *a personal affirmation*. He explicitly states that when he received his calling he "did not immediately consult with anyone" (v. 16), including the apostles (v. 17). Instead, he spent three years in Arabia and Damascus. During this time, Paul sought the Lord's affirmation through personal devotion and solitude. But it was not merely a time of retreat or reflection. It was also his way of assessing his calling through personal experience. Since God had called him to be an apostle to the Gentiles, serving in these areas allowed him to explore and evaluate his calling to preach the gospel to them (see Acts 9:19–25).

In the same way, our calling must be affirmed through our personal experience. The prompting of the Spirit in our hearts through our devotional time will be verified as we begin serving according to our giftedness and calling. His presence and empowerment to fulfill our calling will confirm his will for our lives.

The next step in Paul's experience was *a private affirmation*. Following this season of personal evaluation, Paul sought out Peter (Cephas) in Jerusalem and spent fifteen days with him (v. 18). He also visited with James but did not seek the counsel of any of the other apostles (v. 19–20). In subsequent meetings, Paul makes it clear that he was not seeking their approval or authorization (2:6), although he did receive their affirmation as a fellow apostle (2:7–9).

As you explore your calling, it is necessary and beneficial to consult with other trusted believers who can offer wise counsel. But no one is better positioned to provide personal insight into your calling than someone who is already serving in that capacity. Those who have received a similar or identical calling and have years of experience fulfilling it can help verify your experience. They can also provide you with guidance as you prepare, help you know what to expect, and recommend next steps for you to continue your pursuit.

Finally, the affirmation process includes *a public affirmation*. Paul's ministry had produced evidence of God's favor. He continued to follow the Lord's direction as he traveled to Syria and Cilicia (v. 21). Although he was still unknown to them by sight (v. 22), the word of his ministry preceded his arrival as they marveled, "he who formerly persecuted us now preaches the faith he once tried to destroy" (v. 23). As a result, "they glorified God" because of Paul's witness and service to Christ (v. 24).

Similarly, one of the most important elements of affirming your calling will be the spiritual fruit it produces. Your giftedness and effectiveness will be evident by how God uses your faithfulness in the lives of others. As others are influenced by your service to Christ, God will further confirm your calling. In addition to the personal verification you experience and the testimony of others you influence, godly leaders and spiritually mature believers will also recognize and affirm your giftedness and potential. Their encouragement and affirmation will be instrumental in your growth and confidence in the Lord.

Although these three aspects of affirmation—personal, private, and public—are fundamental to the discernment of any calling, their sequence is not always the same. When I discerned my calling, it was over a period of several months, but these forms of affirmation occurred in the reverse order. Through my voluntary service in the local church, others encouraged me to consider my calling by way of public affirmation. Then those who served in ministry offered me insights and counsel as private affirmation. Finally, through my devotional time with the Lord, these insights were personally affirmed. Your calling will also include each of these three essential steps of affirmation, and its certainty will be solidified through their consideration.

Living It Out

As we devote ourselves to answering God's call on our lives, we can confirm it through the authenticity of our calling as we receive it from Christ and it results in change. We can submit to the authority of our calling as we recognize it as God's divine plan, empowered by his strength, to accomplish his purpose. And we can find assurance in the affirmation of our calling as we verify it personally, privately, and publicly.

Yet confirming our calling also requires us to wrestle with some hard realities of life. We fear failure; we are overwhelmed by the magnitude of serving God; and we are painfully aware of our weaknesses. These realities led Moses to try to convince God to choose someone else for his calling, pleading, "Please, Lord, send someone else" (Exod 4:13). But God's persistence in calling Moses and his faithfulness to use him can help us to overcome the reservations of our hearts.

God's Presence Overcomes Our Inadequacy. When God first called him to be the deliverer of his people, Moses responded with the same question we often ask, "Who am I that I should go?" (Exod 3:11). Moses knew his past. He had killed an Egyptian. He had run from his problems and fled to the wilderness (2:14–15). He was not courageous; he was a coward! But God did not respond by attempting to convince Moses that he was somehow qualified or simply needed more self-confidence. Instead, he assured him, "I will certainly be with you" (3:12). God's identity and his sufficiency as the great "I AM" would be the source of Moses's strength and success (3:14). In the same way, fulfilling our calling does not depend on who we are, but on who he is! When we feel alone and inadequate for our calling, we can remember that he will be with us (Heb 13:5; Isa 43:1–3). When we feel like a nobody, we can rest on the fact that he is the ultimate somebody, the great I AM. And he has called *us* to serve him!

God's Promise Overcomes Our Insecurity. Moses struggled with self-doubt. Any confidence he had based on his previous status in Pharaoh's house or his ability to confront an Egyptian guard had been deflated long ago. His insecurity was revealed through his next response to God, "What if they won't believe me?" (Exod 4:1). But, similar to Jeremiah and Paul's recognition later, God had chosen Moses for this calling from his mother's womb, long before he ever knew it. The Lord's miraculous protection from Pharaoh's execution of the Hebrew babies (2:1–10), his provision for Moses when he fled to Midian (2:11–22), and his preparation of Moses as he shepherded Jethro's flock (3:1) had all been in anticipation of fulfilling God's call on his life. What Moses viewed as random circumstances and personal failures had blended into paralyzing fear. Yet they were actually the providential opportunities God had woven together into his master plan for Moses's life. At the right time, he would use Moses to be his messenger. Just as he overcame Moses's insecurities by promising to accomplish spiritual wonders through him (4:2–9), God can overcome our emotional apprehensions with the reassurance of his desire and willingness to use us.

God's Power Overcomes Our Inability. Moses continued to wrestle with his calling, and his next response revealed his personal inability. He was not simply making an excuse. In a moment of desperate transparency, Moses pleaded with God, "Please, Lord, I have never been eloquent . . . because my mouth and my tongue are sluggish" (4:10). But God reassured Moses that success in his calling would not be dependent on his ability. The Lord reminded Moses that he is the one who has the power to make someone speak, assuring him, "I will help you speak and I will teach you what to say" (4:12). More than anyone else, we are painfully aware of our own inabilities. But God's strength is perfected in our weakness, and his power is displayed through our reliance on him (2 Cor 12:9). Therefore, the only ability God is concerned with is our availability!

Our relationship with God, from our conversion to our calling, is never about our personal ability or adequacy. It's only through Christ's atonement that we are accepted. It's only through his sacrifice that we are made sufficient. And it's only through his grace that we are gifted. In Jesus, we have everything we need to fulfill our calling (2 Pet 1:3). Therefore, we can embrace our calling with confidence, not because of our capability, but because of Christ!

CHAPTER 2

Clarifying God's Call on Your Life

On Christmas morning when I was eight years old, along with my favorite gum, some candy, and a customary pair of socks, I found a notepad in my stocking. It had my favorite team on it, the Duke Blue Devils, and each page was covered with grid lines. It wasn't the most exciting gift I had ever received, but I did find a creative way to enjoy it. I began to use the lines to carefully trace out mazes similar to those you would find on a kids' menu at a restaurant. Eventually I graduated to full-size sheets of graph paper and designed intricate labyrinths with the goal of creating the most confusing mazes with as many dead ends as possible. Drawing them was a lot of work, but it was so entertaining to watch my parents and friends attempt to navigate their way through them and repeatedly have to backtrack and start over.

When it comes to God's will for our lives, many Christians approach it with a similar perspective. We are often convinced that God has designed a plan for us with lots of dead ends as though we are mice making our way through some experimental maze. Whenever we come to a point when we don't know which way to go, we are forced to reverse course and pursue a different direction. This results in us wandering through life with uncertainty, second-guessing our decisions, feeling frustrated at every "wrong turn," and hoping that somehow we will reach our destination and finally find God's will.

But God's will for our lives was never intended to be a maze. He designed it to be amazing! As we answer God's call on our lives and begin to follow his path, how can we know with certainty what his will is for us? Paul answers that question through his prayer for God's people in his letter to the Colossians. This passage teaches us how we can determine God's will for our lives and the necessary steps to fulfill it.

> **Colossians 1:9–12:** [9]For this reason also, since the day we heard this, we haven't stopped praying for you. We are asking that you may be filled with the knowledge of his will in all wisdom and spiritual understanding, [10]so that you may walk worthy of the Lord, fully pleasing to him: bearing fruit in every good work and growing in the knowledge of God, [11]being strengthened with all power, according to his glorious might, so that you may have great endurance and patience, joyfully [12]giving thanks to the Father, who has enabled you to share in the saints' inheritance in the light.

The Possibility of Finding God's Will

One of the most significant aspects of Paul's prayer for the Colossians is found in the request itself. He prays that God's people "may be filled with the knowledge of his will" (v. 9). The implied truth underlying his petition is that it is possible for believers to know and understand God's will for our lives. If it was not a possibility, Paul would not have prayed this for them. Since it *is* achievable, how can we know what God's desire is for our lives?

Most people take a "discovery" approach to determining God's will for their lives. Like a tourist on a beach looking for lost treasures, we approach it with a spiritual metal detector, sweeping it around as we wander through life hoping we stumble onto it: beep . . . . . beep . . . . beep . . . beep . . . beep . . . beep . . . beep . . beep . . beep . . beep. beep.beep.beep!!! Except that when we uncover what we have found, we are often disappointed with what compares to empty cans, tarnished objects, or worthless trinkets. So just like a dead end in the maze, we start the discovery cycle over again hoping that the next "beep" will be it.

But God didn't design his will to be found that way. He wouldn't design a plan for our lives to hide it from us. So we must adopt more of a "discernment" approach. His will for us is outlined with clear instructions, more like a treasure map than a metal detector. Instead of aimlessly wandering around, he gives us the specific steps that will lead us right to the place in life where we can enjoy the satisfying pleasures of knowing him and fully experiencing his will.

These steps are clearly prescribed in Scripture. In fact, at least five times in the New Testament, God's will for us is explicitly stated. First Timothy 2:3–4 teaches us that *it is God's will for us to be saved*. His desire for our salvation affirms his love for all people and his desire for their repentance and redemption (cf. 2 Pet 3:9). Our spiritual conversion is the first step in experiencing God's will for our lives. Paul's prayer acknowledges this in that our "knowledge of his will" is discerned with "wisdom and spiritual understanding" (Col 1:9). But it also demonstrates the reality that, just like salvation, God's will and desire for us can be rejected.

Scripture also affirms that *it is God's will for us to be sanctified*. First Thessalonians 4:3 clearly asserts, "This is God's will [for your life], your sanctification." To be sanctified literally means to be "set apart" or to "be made holy." This is often understood as the process of our lives being conformed to the likeness of Jesus (Rom 8:29). God saves us so that we would become "holy and blameless" before

23

him (Eph 1:4). Therefore, his will for our lives includes our spiritual growth as we are transformed by his grace (2 Cor 3:18).

But the process of sanctification is possible only through another aspect of his will for our lives. The Bible makes it clear that *it is God's will for us to be Spirit-filled.* Paul counseled the Ephesians to "understand what the Lord's will is" and "be filled by the Spirit" (Eph 5:17–18). Although believers receive the Holy Spirit at salvation (Eph 1:13), yielding to his control and allowing him to permeate every area of our lives is an ongoing and deliberate process. Moment-by-moment surrender to his abiding presence is an essential part of God's will for every believer.

As we faithfully live for Christ through the power of the Spirit, we begin to recognize that *it is God's will for us to stand.* First Peter 2:15 teaches, "It is God's will that you silence the ignorance of foolish people by doing good." Living in opposition to a world that is hostile to Christ and his ways requires believers to stand firm in our faith and devotion to him (1 Cor 15:58). This involves taking a stand against the enemy (Eph 6:11–14), standing up for the truth (Jude 1:3), and standing up for those who cannot stand for themselves (Jas 1:27).

Finally, his Word teaches us that *it is God's will for us to suffer.* This isn't what typically comes to mind at graduation celebrations when we are being lavished with well-meaning assurances of the great life that God has for us. It certainly isn't what we visualize as we dream of God's best. But 1 Pet 4:19 tells us that believers "who suffer according to God's will" should continue to trust the Lord and live by obedient faith. This type of suffering is the natural result of God's people "going against the grain," living counterculturally and experiencing resistance and opposition for their faith. Jesus prepared his followers with a warning about this hostility (John 15:18–21). Likewise, Paul instructed Timothy, "all who want to live a godly life in Christ Jesus will be persecuted" (2 Tim 3:12). As followers of Christ, we are not guaranteed to be spared from suffering. In fact, we are assured of the opposite. When we live according to his will, we have to endure hardship for his name's sake.

Because these five aspects of God's will are clearly stated in the Scriptures, none of us has to wonder blindly, what is God's will for my life? He has told us. Granted, these elements of God's will do not specifically tell us what college we should choose, what career path to follow, whom we should marry, or whether we should buy the new car we want. But these elements are even better! They are clear. We know with certainty that it's what God wants. They are consistent. They won't change tomorrow even if our circumstances do. And they are customized. Even though they are universally true, they are personal instructions and applicable for each one of us.

But these spiritual realities of God's will are also practical. When we devote ourselves to pursuing these things that God has clearly revealed, his more specific will for our lives will be realized. Consider the movie *The Karate Kid*, not the remake, the original. The main character, Daniel-son, convinces Mr. Miyagi, a repairman at his apartment complex, to teach him martial arts so that he can defend himself against the spoiled troublemakers who have been bullying him as the new kid in school. But his newly recruited sensei doesn't take him to work out in a dojo; he brings him to his house and enlists him to do seemingly random chores—washing and waxing cars, sanding his outside floors, staining his fence, and painting his house. He gives him specific instructions of how he wants each task performed. It doesn't take long for Daniel to get upset. After several days of exhausting work, he threatens to quit. At that point, Mr. Miyagi demonstrates, in dramatic Hollywood fashion, how all of these skills make him into a karate expert! Using his "chore techniques," he's blocking punches and thwarting kicks as if he's been training for years!

When it comes to discerning God's will, there are some more realistic parallels. When we obey his clearly expressed desires and specific instructions, they ultimately translate into a knowledge and understanding of his intentions for our lives. By devoting ourselves entirely to those aspects of his will that he has plainly revealed, we will be able to discern the more personalized and specific plans he has for us. As a result, we can move forward with confidence, being convinced that it is possible to know and understand God's will for our lives.

The Purpose of Following God's Will

Paul's prayer for the Colossians not only reveals the possibility of knowing God's will, it also challenges us to embrace the purpose of following God's will. Notice what he goes on to pray, "so that you may walk worthy of the Lord, fully pleasing to him" (Col 1:10). Paul's desire for them to know God's will is not for their own personal knowledge or fulfillment. His purpose is so that their lives may be pleasing to God!

We must adopt this same purpose. Let's be honest: most of the time we desire to discern God's will for our own personal benefit. Of course we want to honor the Lord, but really we are seeking to know his will for selfish reasons. We want our lives to be fully pleasing to *us*. "God, I'll do what you want me to do as long as it makes *me* happy, as long as it fits in *my* plans, as long as it achieves *my* dreams, answers *my* prayers, and satisfies *my* desires!" But Paul's prayer radically changes our goal for discerning God's will. It's so our lives will be "fully pleasing to *him*."

In other words, for us to accomplish his will, *we must long to please Christ*. Satisfying him must become our deepest passion and our highest goal. To pursue his will for our lives, we must be willing to lay down our dreams and desires. God does not always ask us to relinquish these things, but he knows our hearts and whether or not we are willing to do so. It is much easier to say that we will, but when it comes down to it, are we willing to lay anything and everything on the altar for him?! Many people expect the Lord to give them what they desire, and some may even quote Ps 37:4 to justify their expectations: "Take delight in the LORD, and he will give you your heart's desires." But this understanding portrays God as some cosmic genie who is obligated to grant us our wishes as long as we ask "in Jesus's name." What this verse actually means is that God will infuse our hearts with his desires when we learn to delight ourselves in what pleases him.

But our desire to please Christ cannot simply be a sentiment or feeling; it must translate into action. We must not only long to please Christ; *we must live to please Christ*. Notice again in verse 10, the purpose given for discerning God's will was so that the Colossians would "walk worthy of the Lord." This describes our lifestyle, our personal relationships, and our ambitions and goals. It means that our lives must be entirely and exclusively devoted to honoring him. We can't live the way we want to and hide behind sanctified excuses, such as "Well, God knows my heart." Our true desires will be revealed through our behavior.

Early in my seminary days, I met a guy named Mike. He was studying to earn a ministry degree, but he didn't believe that God had called him to be a pastor. From his childhood, Mike had aspired to be in law enforcement. He had devoted his entire life to achieving his goal, and prior to coming to seminary he had accomplished it. Mike became a United States Secret Service agent. While serving in this capacity, he sensed God leading him in a different direction. Reluctantly Mike quit his job and moved back home to work as a local law enforcement officer while he figured things out. He continued to devote himself to following the Lord and still could not find peace. So, believing God had called him to go to seminary, Mike resigned again and trusted the Lord to reveal his plan.

For more than three years as a student, Mike worked for campus services doing maintenance. The odd jobs and minimal pay wasn't what he was used to and certainly wasn't what he had envisioned for his life. Until one day, not long before Mike was set to graduate, the president of the seminary called him in for a meeting. He described for Mike his vision to implement a security strategy for the campus. There would need to be measures taken to protect the faculty and students, guidelines and procedures established and put in place, a staff hired, including someone to oversee it all. The head of campus security would be provided with a service vehicle and an official position with the local police department as a full-fledged officer and chaplain for their force. It was a job tailor-made for Mike, and the president offered it to him on the spot! More than fifteen years later, he still serves in this capacity.

Mike's story is rare, but it's not unique. I'm convinced the reason we don't hear more of these types of testimonies is because most believers aren't willing to embrace *pleasing Christ* as the purpose of following God's will. We are really pursuing it for selfish reasons. The job God had for Mike didn't even exist when he laid down his dreams and went to seminary. But if we will devote ourselves to pleasing him, we can trust that he has a plan that fully accounts for the skills and passions he ingrained within our hearts when he created us.

So why do you want to know God's will? Is it for you? Or is it for him? Scripture clearly teaches that our purpose for following his will should ultimately be to please him.

The Process of Fulfilling God's Will

Paul's prayer for Colossian believers also includes a picture of what our lives will look like when we are living in a way that pleases and honors him. In the rest of this passage (vv. 10–12), Paul identifies four ongoing actions that describe the Lord's work in our lives as we surrender to his will. These parallel phrases help us to recognize what the process of fulfilling God's will involves.

The first aspect of the process that Paul identifies, "bearing fruit in every good work" (v. 10), teaches us that *we are called to good works*. Genuine faith inevitably produces good works (Jas 2:14–26), and God has redeemed us to be a people who are zealous for good works (Titus 2:14). These works are "fruit" produced by the Spirit (Gal 5:22–23) that glorifies God and distinguishes us as Jesus's disciples (John 15:8). As part of God's will for our lives, he has prepared good works for us to do (Eph 2:10), and he enables us to perform them (Phil 2:13).

The process of fulfilling God's will also includes "growing in the knowledge of God" (v. 10). This means that *we are called to go deep*. Our relationship with the Lord is intended to increase in spiritual depth and personal intimacy (2 Pet 3:18). Just as Paul elevated knowing Christ above everything else (Phil 3:8), we must also set this as our ultimate goal and highest priority. We grow in our knowledge of him through devotional time in prayer, personal Bible study, and faithful obedience. These disciplines not only enable us to discern his will, they also equip us to fulfill it (Rom 12:2).

29

Paul also points out that *we are called to grow strong*. The process of fulfilling God's will involves "being strengthened with all power, according to his glorious might" (v. 11). This is not merely encouragement for us to rely on the Lord. It means that fulfilling God's plan will be impossible apart from his divine strength. God's will for our lives will extend us beyond our own capabilities. It will require emotional and physical stamina that can only be sustained with his spiritual strength (cf. Eph 3:16). But by his might, the Lord will empower us to have "great endurance and patience" (v. 11). If we pursue a path that can be accomplished in our own strength and ability, then we have achieved something less than God's will.

Finally, the process of fulfilling God's will involves living with gratitude. *We are called to give thanks*. Paul's instructions conclude with us "giving thanks to the Father" (v. 12). The culmination of our devotion to God's plan is a joyful and grateful heart. The privilege of participating in the Lord's kingdom enterprise is possible only because he "has enabled us to share in the saints' inheritance in the light" (v. 12). God graciously includes us and willingly uses us to accomplish his divine purposes here on earth. Therefore, we should "give thanks in everything; for this is God's will for [us] in Christ Jesus" (1 Thess 5:18). When we are mindful of the Lord's undeserved kindness toward us, it should influence everything we do, saturating our hearts and lives with gratitude (Col 3:17).

Living It Out

It is clear from Paul's prayer for the Colossians that we can know and understand God's will for our lives based on what he has already revealed to us. It is also obvious that following his will requires a radical shift in perspective that pursues God's will for his pleasure, not ours. When we adopt this mind-set, we can devote ourselves to following his plan and watching him work in and through our lives.

These truths provide assurance, confidence, and direction, but they can also leave us asking the practical question, so where do I begin? If we embrace the truths of Colossians 1, what are the initial steps we should take to begin finding, following, and fulfilling God's will for our lives? There are three necessary steps that can initiate your journey no matter where your starting point is.

✳ *Step 1: Purify Yourself.* Whenever we need to seek God's direction for our lives, it must always begin by opening the eyes and ears of our hearts. This means that we must confess and repent of any known sin in our lives. Attempting to follow God's voice with sin remaining in our hearts is like trying to listen to someone talk with cotton stuffed in our ears. We can hear the sound, but the voice is muffled. God is constantly speaking to his children, guiding us with his wise counsel and directing us according to his perfect plan. But many times we are unable to discern what he is saying, because we fail to remove the deafening earwax of sin that's clogging our spiritual ears. Like the psalmist, we should invite God to search our hearts and investigate our lives for any offenses that are remaining so that he can cleanse us through the blood of his Son and lead us according to his will (Ps 139:23–24). We must be willing to turn from those things that hinder our ability to hear his voice. Likewise, in turn, we must devote ourselves to those things that please and honor him.

✳ *Step 2: Position Yourself.* Oftentimes we desire to hear God speak, but we aren't in a position to hear him. God primarily speaks to us through his Word and to our hearts by his Spirit. This means that to hear his voice we must position ourselves before him in prayer and devotional Bible study. If we are not spending time in his presence, we should not expect to hear him speak. But the Lord also speaks to us through his people. Other believers are often used as God's messengers to speak truth into our lives, to offer us godly advice, and to help us discern his will. But their counsel should always be tested before it is trusted. We must measure it by the objective truth of Scripture, making sure it corresponds with and never contradicts God's Word. Positioning ourselves in these ways gives us the opportunity to hear God when and where he speaks.

✳ **Step 3:** *Prepare yourself.* As we discern God's will, we cannot sit back and passively expect it to be accomplished. We must devote ourselves to spiritually and practically preparing for what he has in store. We don't know God's timeline, but it's likely that he won't reveal his plan to us until we are ready. This means that oftentimes when we feel as if we are waiting on the Lord, he may actually be waiting on us. Therefore, while we are prayerfully considering God's direction, we must wholeheartedly devote ourselves to spiritual intimacy and maturity. Developing spiritual disciplines, growing in our faith, building up our spiritual stamina, and living with expectancy and hope—all can be a necessary part of our preparation.

Another aspect of preparing ourselves involves our service for Christ. As we are pursuing God's will for our lives, we must be active among his people. Ministry involvement in the local church will always be part of his plan for us, regardless of our vocation. His next step for us may be discerned through our participation in the ministries of a family of faith and through the relationships we establish as part of God's body. One common mistake people make when renewing their pursuit of his will is to step back from things they are already doing. But God will lead us forward from where we are. Whatever the last thing is that God told you to do, devote yourself entirely to it.

Preparation for God's call can also include education. When you prayerfully begin to consider formal training for your calling and career, it is important to explore institutions of higher learning that offer programs that correspond to God's will for your life. Schools like The College at Southeastern, Southeastern Baptist Theological Seminary, and Oklahoma Baptist University can offer a well-balanced learning experience that provides training in the foundational disciplines of education as well as in your area of specialization, while teaching them from a distinctively Christian perspective. This can help define your vocational career as your spiritual calling as you prepare to fulfill God's will.

Years ago at the end of a worship service, a young teen came forward with tears streaming down her face. Her typical smile and infectious joy had been replaced with a burden of despair. Through her tears, she expressed her discernment of God's call to missions. She was confused, because at her age she had no idea what that meant. As a young pastor, I responded by conveying the sage advice, "Jody, I'm not sure what that means either." Although I could not provide any specific direction, I encouraged her that, if she would devote herself to preparing for God's will, he would reveal the rest. She did, and so did he. Within weeks, her parents surrendered to full-time missions, and she would spend the majority of her teenage years serving God in East Asia.

If we will begin to prepare ourselves spiritually, as we purify and position ourselves before God, we can trust him to reveal his will for us as he grants us the wisdom to discern it.

PART II

ASSISTING THE CHURCH

G rowing up near the beach, I remember hearing a story of a young man who enjoyed building sand castles. These were not your typical mud and bucket towers. They were elaborate grit palaces fit for imaginary royalty! While he spent hours building these sandy mansions, some of the other local boys found just as much enjoyment in tearing them down. After he finished his construction projects, they would act as human wrecking balls by kicking, stomping, and plowing through the fortresses. The young man grew increasingly frustrated until one day he had had enough.

Following weeks of futile attempts to dissuade them, the young man decided to outsmart them. Before he began constructing his sandcastle, he built a surprise foundation with a few cinderblocks and bricks. Sometime later when he was completing his latest masterpiece, the demolition crew came walking down the beach and spotted the estate. Immediately they sprinted toward the massive sandcastle. As the young man fled down the beach in the opposite direction, he could hear their painful shrieks and tearful screams as they discovered the indestructible core of support. Ouch!!

Similar to these destructive efforts, the church of Jesus Christ has been under attack for the past two thousand years. Outside forces of culture and critics, along with internal disputes and personal disappointments, have attempted to tear down God's people. But

Jesus has established his Church on an immovable foundation that cannot be destroyed. We are his spiritual fortress that he has assembled to advance his kingdom in this world. As God's people, we are called to work together to fulfill his plans. For us personally, this means that his individual will for each of us is part of a bigger Master plan. This also means that his call on your life will be discerned, and ultimately accomplished, through your service as part of his family of faith.

To determine God's plan for the church, and our role in it, we need to make an important distinction. When we speak of the Church (capital C), we are referring to the global church consisting of all Christians everywhere. In this sense, when we trust Christ, we become a member of the universal Church, the spiritual body of believers worldwide operating collectively as God's people. This means that we *are* the Church, and we function as the Church whether we are at work, at school, at home, and anywhere in between. At the same time, the church (little c) is a gathering of believers in a local community who unite together to fulfill God's mission. As a spiritual family in a specific context, Christians in a local church join together to worship, serve, grow, and go. The local church does not exist without the global church, and the global church cannot operate without the local church.

The basis for understanding your personal role and responsibility as part of God's people and his master plan derives from three primary truths and texts that establish the identity, purpose, and mission of the Church.

The Great Confession

Matthew 16:13–18: [13]When Jesus came to the region of Caesarea Philippi, he asked his disciples, "Who do people say that the Son of Man is?"

[14]They replied, "Some say John the Baptist; others, Elijah; still others, Jeremiah or one of the prophets."

[15]"But you," he asked them, "who do you say that I am?"

[16]Simon Peter answered, "You are the Messiah, the Son of the living God."

[17]Jesus responded, "Blessed are you, Simon son of Jonah, because flesh and blood did not reveal this to you, but my Father in heaven. [18]And I also say to you that you are Peter, and on this rock I will build my church, and the gates of Hades will not overpower it."

While Jesus was mentoring his disciples, Jesus was constantly challenging their faith and spiritual awareness. So his question about others' perception of him would not have seemed unusual (v. 13). His disciples' explanation of his public reputation as a prophet or religious leader was also not surprising (v. 14). But Jesus used it to open the door for the real question he wanted them to answer. "Who do you say that I am?" (v. 15). The correct answer would not only serve as a proper affirmation, it would reveal the depth of their personal understanding. Peter responded in faith and spiritual insight, "You are the Messiah, the Son of the living God" (v. 16).

This personal confession is the basis for our relationship with Jesus. Embracing him by faith as our Savior and Lord is the fundamental component of our personal salvation. But Christ's identity is also the foundational truth on which he established the existence of the church, "On this rock I will build my church" (v. 18). Our common faith in Jesus provides the spiritual basis that unites us together as God's people, the "church."

This declaration introduced his followers to their new collective identity. Jesus's pronouncement, "I will build *my* church," also exalts him as the supreme leader and sovereign Lord over his people (see Col 1:18). Additionally, his declaration identifies us as a spiritual entity that he would "build," one that would advance his kingdom, and one that could not be destroyed or overcome (v. 18). Through his sacrificial and substitutionary death on the cross, Jesus purchased us, the church, as his personal possession. We are his body (Eph 4:12–16), his bride (Eph 5:22–33), and his building (1 Cor 3:9–11). And we are established firmly on the immovable and indestructible foundation of Jesus Christ himself!

Our collective identity as the church also determines the nature of our individual identity. We are personally defined by our relationship with Christ as members of his eternal family (1 John 3:1). We call on God as our heavenly Father; other believers are our brothers and sisters in Christ; and we are guaranteed a glorious inheritance (Rom 8:15–17). These truths assure you that he has a plan for your life and that plan will be realized as part of his spiritual family.

The Great Commandment

Matthew 22:34–40: [34]When the Pharisees heard that he had silenced the Sadducees, they came together. [35]And one of them, an expert in the law, asked a question to test him: [36]"Teacher, which command in the law is the greatest?"

[37]He said to him, "Love the Lord your God with all your heart, with all your soul, and with all your mind. [38]This is the greatest and most important command. [39]The second is

like it: Love your neighbor as yourself. [40]All the Law and
the Prophets depend on these two commands."

In the same way that our personal identity as believers and our
collective identity as his church are united by a common foundation,
our individual existence and corporate existence are joined together
by a single purpose. Jesus revealed this purpose in a definitive response to a cynic's question regarding the greatest commandment
(vv. 34–36). The scribe was attempting to measure his faithfulness
by his ability to keep God's standards. He wanted to know which
ones to prioritize. But Jesus replied with God's greatest command,
one that is measured more by the condition of our hearts than the
work of our hands. "Love the Lord your God with all your heart,
with all your soul, and with all your mind" (v. 37).

This was not a new command, it had always been God's primary desire for his people (see Deut 6:5). Jesus identified it as "the
greatest and most important command" because it serves as the root
of all sincere obedience. Without love for God, our good works are
empty attempts to prove ourselves and earn his acceptance. But with
love for him as our motivation, our actions for him will flow from
our affections for him. It is also the greatest commandment because
it is comprehensive. Heart, soul, and mind were not intended to be
categories that compartmentalize our lives. They were meant to reflect the all-encompassing nature of our love for God that should
saturate every aspect of our being.

We must also recognize that our love for God is not expressed
in the typical ways we demonstrate affection in our earthly relationships. We can't send him flowers, take him to eat at a nice restaurant, or buy him expensive jewelry. The Bible says that our love for
God is expressed through obedience (1 John 5:3) and love for others
(1 John 4:20–21). This is why Jesus connected the two commands,

"The second is like it: love your neighbor as yourself" (v. 39). God's greatest expression of love was demonstrated by his sacrifice for humanity (1 John 4:10). Likewise, our greatest expression of love for God will be reflected in our sacrificial love for people.

God's extravagant and relentless love for us compels us to live with reckless abandon for him instead of selfishly living for ourselves (2 Cor 5:14–15). We don't follow his commands out of duty or obligation, but as a display of our love for him and in response to his love for us (1 John 4:19). As we serve the Lord, it is easy to lose sight of this as our primary purpose. But our personal and practical responsibilities can never be detached from the ultimate goal of loving God and loving others. This purpose for you, individually *and* as part of his church, will help to determine your calling and career as you devote yourself to fulfilling the Great Commandment.

The Great Commission

Matthew 28:18–20: [18]Jesus came near and said to them, "All authority has been given to me in heaven and on earth. [19]Go, therefore, and make disciples of all nations, baptizing them in the name of the Father and of the Son and of the Holy Spirit, [20]teaching them to observe everything I have commanded you. And remember, I am with you always, to the end of the age."

Like our identity and purpose, the mission of our individual lives is also inseparable from the mission of the church. Before Jesus ascended to heaven, he asserted his ultimate authority and commissioned his followers (v. 18). The standing order from our risen Lord and Savior was clear and simple, "Make disciples" (v. 19). This is the exclusive command of the Great Commission, and it must govern every ambition in our lives. With "*all* authority" we are commanded to make disciples of "*all* nations" by teaching them to obey *all* things with the assurance that he will be with us at *all* times.

Jesus's supporting instructions provide the strategy for how we will accomplish his mission, by going . . . baptizing . . . and teaching. As we are *going* through life, we must embrace every day, every place, every task, and every person as an opportunity to fulfill our mission to make disciples. This means that everything from routine visits to the grocery store to our career aspirations, whether in a secular or sacred capacity, must be approached from a missional perspective. We are always on mission! Making disciples also includes *baptizing* them. This involves inviting others to trust Christ for salvation, to unite their lives with his, and to be assimilated into his family of faith, the church. *Teaching* them requires us to invest in others as we relationally lead them to grow in Christlikeness through obedience and faithfulness. We must become disciples who make disciples!

The mission of God's church must be embraced as your personal mission. The magnitude of the mission seems far greater than anything you can accomplish on your own, and it is. But your life, your calling, and your gifts and abilities are all part of God's master plan that he weaves together with other believers to accomplish his kingdom purposes. You also have his promise that he will be with you to guide you, to provide for you, to protect you, and to empower you to accomplish everything he has called you to do (v. 20). As a follower of Jesus and a member of the body of Christ, your mission is clear. He has commanded you by his authority, commissioned you as his agent, and comforted you with his assurance. You are called to make disciples.

Looking Ahead

In this section, we will consider God's plan for you as a member of the local church with the broader understanding of your life as part of the global church as well. Every one of us is a specific and strategic member of the body of Christ and plays an important role in God's plan (Eph 4:16). God has specifically called you to serve his kingdom and has provided you with the necessary gifts to accomplish his purpose for your life. The chapters in this section will help you to understand your role in his mission and your responsibility as a member of his family.

CHAPTER 3

God Enlists Us in His Service

H ave you ever heard the phrase "drawing a line in the sand"? Some people associate this with a threat, daring you to cross the line and face the consequences. Others use the saying as a caution of a different kind, warning you of a trap; if you cross the line, you won't be able to escape or return. But perhaps the most recognizable use of the phrase derives from a historical event in United States history.

During the Texas revolution, one of the most famous clashes between Texan and Mexican forces was the battle of the Alamo. On March 6, 1836, the Mexican army, led by General Santa Anna, advanced on the compound and seized control. The surviving Texas soldiers had retreated into the inner buildings with their commander, Col. William Travis. With the Mexican victory all but certain, General Santa Anna sent a messenger to Travis demanding the surrender of the defense forces or threatening their execution. According to legend, Colonel Travis pulled his unit together and explained the hopeless situation. Choosing to die rather than surrender, the colonel pulled his battle sword and, "drawing a line in the sand," invited any and all willing soldiers to join him in fighting to the death for the sake of the cause. All but one of the soldiers would join Travis. Although he and his remaining troops died, their sacrifice and resolve—along with the phrase "Remember the Alamo"—would inspire the Texan forces, leading them to ultimate victory.

For Colonel Travis, drawing a line in the sand wasn't a threat or a trap, it was a threshold. Crossing the line would be an irreversible decision that they would unite with their leader to follow him into battle. In the same way, when Jesus calls us to follow him, he is not daring us or warning us. He is inviting us to join him, to pledge our allegiance to the cause of his eternal kingdom, and to sacrifice everything to unite with him. The victory is already won; he defeated the enemy when he died on the cross, paying the debt for our sin (Col 2:14–15), and rose again to conquer death and the grave (1 Cor 15:55–57). By joining him, we are surrendering our lives to his control and his cause. We are enlisted in his service and must seek to please our commanding officer (2 Tim 2:4). There are three primary truths Jesus wants us to understand to live a life devoted to his cause. Jesus outlined them in a familiar teaching.

Matthew 5:13–16: [13]You are the salt of the earth. But if the salt should lose its taste, how can it be made salty? It's no longer good for anything but to be thrown out and trampled under people's feet.

[14]You are the light of the world. A city situated on a hill cannot be hidden. [15]No one lights a lamp and puts it under a basket, but rather on a lampstand, and it gives light for all who are in the house. [16]In the same way, let your light shine before others, so that they may see your good works and give glory to your Father in heaven.

The Distinct Identity of the Believer

Jesus's expectations and instructions for his followers are rooted in their relationship with him. In this passage, he redefines our identity by drawing a sharp distinction between us and our culture. His use of "salt *of the earth*" and "light *of the world*" distinguishes us from those who don't know him. Simply put, we are different. This is not merely describing a contrast in our spiritual beliefs or religious behavior. The metaphorical phrases "you *are* the salt" and "you *are* the light" speak to our unique nature as his disciples. These word pictures also provide insight into the type of distinction we are meant to exhibit.

Salt is a natural preservative and purifying agent. Scripture teaches us that the world and its desires are passing away (1 John 2:15–17). Our presence within the world serves as a countermeasure, one that preserves goodness and promotes virtue. The culture is deteriorating, its moral fabric eroding, and as believers our presence is intended to sustain what remains. Salt is also a sanitizing agent, one that disinfects by means of its purity. Christ redeemed us "to cleanse for himself a people of his own possession, eager to do good works" (Titus 2:14). Our existence as salt adds a distinct flavor to the world, one that is savory and desirable, and one that preserves and purifies.

Similarly, our distinction as light is just as drastic. The brilliance of light radiates against the darkness of the world around us (Phil 2:14–15). Light exposes the filth of sin and convicts it with heat (John 3:19–21). At the same time, it guides the follower (John 8:12), directing others to the loving Father who called us "out of darkness into his marvelous light" (1 Pet 2:9). Our presence as light in the world distinguishes us as Christ's followers, counteracting the pervading darkness that cannot overcome his illuminating presence (John 1:5).

Our distinct identity is evident to us as we struggle against temptation while others indulge in it and relish in immorality. Our unique nature makes us uncomfortable when we are immersed in a culture drowning in sin that celebrates its own depravity. As believers who have God's indwelling presence through his Spirit, we grieve him when we sin and our hearts are convicted (Eph 4:30). And when we stand for righteousness and live a godly life, we are persecuted by our culture (2 Tim 3:12). But be encouraged. All of these things signify that you are different. You are not like the world. You are salt. You are light. It's your nature, your distinct identity in Christ.

The Dangerous Influence of the World

Although his use of *salt* and *light* speak to our distinct identity, it also makes a statement about the nature of the lost world around us. Our identity as salt implies that the culture is spiritually diseased and decaying. Our association with light implies that others exist in a state of darkness and deception. Although our distinction is one of essence that cannot be altered, our distinction can be diminished by the dangerous influence of the world.

Jesus warned his followers of this possibility when he cautioned them, "If the salt should lose its taste. . . ." He doesn't imply that it can lose its unique nature, just as we can't lose our salvation. But when blended with impurities, the salt can lose its distinction. When salt no longer is pure, when it can no longer preserve without contaminating, "It's no longer good for anything but to be thrown out and trampled under people's feet." We, like salt, can become corrupted. When we allow the sinfulness of the world to permeate our hearts, we become polluted by the world (Jas 1:27). Gradually our hearts corrode from the inside out. Like salt air that comes in contact with metal and produces rust, when we let the filth of the world infiltrate our hearts it corrupts and deteriorates our saltiness.

Just as salt can be corrupted, our light can be concealed. Jesus cautioned that the dangerous influence of the world can hide our light or put "it under a basket." This occurs when our behavior begins to blend in with those around us. We become camouflaged; even though our light cannot be extinguished, its radiance becomes diminished. When our lives are veiled with worldliness, we are no longer the city that is set apart on a hill that "cannot be hidden." As light, we are intended to shine with a heavenly righteousness. A godly and honorable lifestyle distinguishes us from our culture and reflects to a dark and dying world the kindness and holiness of Jesus.

The dangerous influence of the culture requires us to guard ourselves in order to maintain our distinction and avoid its corruptive, corrosive, and concealing effects. We must limit our exposure to sinful pressures and pleasures. The places we go, the things we watch and listen to, and the people we associate with, can all have devastating impacts on our lives and testimonies.

Your ability to fulfill God's plan for your life will directly correspond with your ability to protect yourself from the dangerous influence of the world. Scripture warns, "Do not be deceived: 'Bad company corrupts good morals'" (1 Cor 15:33). God's Word also teaches us that "friendship with the world," adopting its values and virtues, constitutes spiritual adultery and puts us at odds with him (Jas 4:4). Beware of the enemy. He is real. And he is seeking to destroy you (John 10:10) and devour you (1 Pet 5:8).

47

The Desired Impact for the Lord

Our distinction as salt and light is not only one of essence; it is intended to be one of impact. God never intended us to be different simply for the sake of being different. He desires our lives to be distinct in order to *make* a difference. Jesus implies our desired impact when he describes the salt that loses its saltiness, "It's no longer good for anything." In other words, when we lose our distinction, we cannot be used to accomplish our intended purpose. He describes the impact of the lamp in a positive manner, "It gives light for all who are in the house." Clearly Jesus intends for our light to provide illumination for others, "In the same way, let your light shine before others."

The distinction of our lives as salt and light becomes evident when others taste and see our "good works" (v. 16). This phrase describes the practical difference that our essential distinction should make. Many times as Christians we are careful to avoid the phrase, *good works*, because Scripture is so clear that our salvation occurs apart from any effort or work on our part. No one can be justified, or declared righteous, before God and accepted by him on the basis of good works (Rom 3:20). It is only by grace through faith in Christ that we are saved, "not from works" (Eph 2:8–9).

Although we are right to avoid any implication that would associate works with receiving salvation, Scripture is also clear that good works are evidence, and the expected outcome, of our salvation. Genuine faith in Christ that saves us will manifest itself by the good works it produces in our lives (Jas 2:14–26). Jesus redeemed us and set us apart as his people who would be zealous for good works (Titus 2:14). In fact, the same passage that teaches us that we are saved only by grace through faith concludes by affirming, "For we are his workmanship, created in Christ Jesus *for good works*, which God prepared ahead of time for us to do" (Eph 2:10).

These are the good works that Jesus describes as the natural effect of our distinct identities as salt and light. They stand out in our culture as a moral, wholesome, and virtuous lifestyle. They are also demonstrated through the kindness, love, and mercy that we extend to others around us. They are tangible acts of charity and goodness, efforts to serve others and meet their needs. In our daily lives, they are also reflected in our dedication and devotion, our effort and endurance, as we fulfill our responsibilities in our homes, our schools, our jobs, and our churches. And, most important, our good works are the embodiment of Christ himself as we live for him and are conformed to his image.

Our good works are meant to make a difference simply through the actions we perform. As a result of our efforts, the lives of people around us will be influenced. Although this is the most direct impact, it is not the ultimate goal. Jesus teaches us that our good works are performed so that others may see them "and give glory to your Father in heaven" (Matt 5:16). In other words, our efforts are not meant to call attention to ourselves. We don't live virtuous lives to be esteemed by others or to elevate ourselves above them. Our lives of faithfulness and obedience are intended to glorify God!

As his earthly ministry was nearing its completion, Jesus prayed, "I have glorified you on the earth by completing the work you gave me to do" (John 17:4). Similarly, God is glorified by our lives when we fulfill his will and accomplish his plan for us. Glorifying him is achieved in several ways. First, we exalt him through our submission and obedience. A surrendered heart magnifies his supremacy and sovereignty. Second, faithfulness to his will and his ways honors him with love and devotion, that which reflects his unrelenting affection for us. Third, selfless service and sacrifice for

Christ and for others glorifies him by embodying the gospel, that is God willingly offering his own Son on our behalf. Finally, God is glorified by our lives when we give praise and thanks to him, not only through familiar forms of worship but in everyday conversations and lifestyle expressions.

The ultimate purpose God has for each of us is to glorify him. His plan for you—your education, your family, your calling, and your ministry—is intended to bring glory to his name. Therefore, you must adopt this as your chief ambition, superseding every other desire and submitting every other goal to this supreme purpose.

Living It Out

Jesus taught his disciples these truths in the midst of the most powerful and practical sermon ever preached, the Sermon on the Mount (Matthew 5–7). These principles extend beyond this particular passage and permeate his entire message. Similarly, they're meant to expand beyond guiding principles and saturate our daily lives. In his sermon, Jesus expounds on these truths, combines them with practical instruction, and teaches us three fundamental desires God has for each of us.

A Life That Satisfies Us. Does God want us to be happy? Yes! Absolutely. There's no doubt. Jesus describes, and prescribes, a life for his followers that is "blessed" (5:3–11). He intends for our lives to be full of gladness and rejoicing (5:12), blessing and reward (6:4, 6, 16), and he promises to provide for us according to our needs (6:33; 7:7–11). The life God has for you will bring you the deepest satisfaction, the greatest depth of fulfillment, and a level of contentment that you could never experience apart from him.

But we must recognize that the peace, satisfaction, and fulfillment God offers us is not what we typically associate with happiness.

It is not simply an emotional feeling or a temporary euphoria that is experienced through worldly pleasures. It is not enthusiasm or excitement that comes from the accumulation of riches, material possessions, or earthly fame. But his joy and satisfaction exceeds all of these things in infinite measure.

The contentment Jesus provides for us, true joy and happiness, can be experienced only through our relationship with him. Jesus does not promise us joy through a life free from hardship or heartache (5:12); rather, it is found through the abundant life he offers (John 10:10). This means that God is more concerned with our holiness than he is our happiness. The fullness of joy in this life is found through obedience to his Word and faithfulness to him (John 15:10–11). He designed you, gifted you, created your preferences, and is fully aware of your life's circumstances. He knows better than anyone, including you, what will satisfy your deepest desires. In the ultimate sense, Jesus himself is the source of true satisfaction. "In your presence is abundant joy; at your right hand are eternal pleasures" (Ps 16:11). As you fulfill his will, find your joy in Christ.

A Life That Testifies to Others. While Jesus desires our deep and personal satisfaction, he also intends for our lives to influence those around us. When God uses us in the lives of others, it heightens our sense of fulfillment as we achieve the influential purpose he intends for us. As we saw in our study of the salt-and-light passage, God wants to make a difference *in* our lives so that he can make a difference *through* our lives. But these verses are not the only place in the Sermon on the Mount that Jesus teaches this truth. Throughout his sermon, Jesus describes how he desires to use us to show and share his love.

When we faithfully follow Christ, others will see our "good works" and our lives will serve as a testimony for him (Matt 5:16). Our obedience to his Word and faithful teaching instructs others to seek and serve the Lord (5:19). When we live with integrity and show kindness to others, it identifies us as his children (5:45–48). And a life of humble devotion is ultimately displayed through genuine acts of righteousness that honor him, not actions motivated by public recognition (6:1–2, 5, 16). Sincere acts of personal dedication immerse us in his love so that we can share his love with others. As he extends his kindness to us, we are called to extend that kindness to others, treating them as we desire to be treated (7:11–12).

God will use our faithfulness to testify to others on his behalf. Therefore, we must view our calling and approach our vocation as a ministry for his sake. Personal ambition can never be our motivation. Instead, we must "do nothing out of selfish ambition or conceit, but in humility consider others more important than [ourselves]," not looking out for our own interests, but for the interests of others (Phil 2:3–4).

A Life That Glorifies Him. God's desire for our personal satisfaction and spiritual impact serves an even greater purpose, one beyond ourselves. Ultimately our lives are not about us at all; they are meant to bring glory to him. Scripture instructs us, "Whatever you do, do everything for the glory of God" (1 Cor 10:31). The life Jesus described in the Sermon on the Mount expounds on the desired impact he specified, "that they may see your good works and give glory to your Father in heaven" (5:16).

As we demonstrate the forgiveness, integrity, kindness, generosity, and other qualities Jesus prescribed in his sermon, we are embodying the attributes of God. In doing so, God's glory is manifested and magnified as his character is revealed through our obedience to him. God is glorified by our lives when we actively and accurately reflect his nature. Therefore, as you follow and fulfill his will, you must devote yourself to faithfully representing the Lord.

God is also glorified by the honor and praise he receives from our lives. We are often tempted to take credit for what God accomplishes in and through us. But we must be careful to recognize his goodness and grace as the basis for anything that we are able to achieve. Therefore, we must "continually offer up to God a sacrifice of praise, that is, the fruit of lips that confess his name" (Heb 13:15). In addition to giving him the glory, we must also point others to do the same. Just as no one marvels at the brush used to paint the Sistine Chapel, we are not intended to be the objects of people's praise or adoration. It's the artist, not the instrument, who is heralded for the extraordinary feats he accomplishes by ordinary means. "For from him and through him and to him are all things. To him be the glory forever" (Rom 11:36).

When Jesus draws a line in the sand, it is an invitation to live a life that satisfies us, testifies to others, and glorifies him. As you find, follow, and fulfill his will, do so with the confident assurance and personal guidance that these truths can provide for you, remembering to "seek first the kingdom of God and his righteousness, and all these things will be provided for you" (Matt 6:33).

CHAPTER 4

God Equips Us For His Service

A li Hafed, an ancient Persian, possessed great wealth. He owned acres of farmland with fruitful orchards, elaborate gardens, and fields of grain. His peaceful life was interrupted one day when he welcomed a guest who told him of a different kind of riches. He described to Hafed the rarest and most precious of gems—diamonds. He told him of their beauty and their value. As a result, Hafed grew discontent with his possessions. He decided he would sell his farm and devote his life to searching for diamonds.

The wealthy Persian spent all of his resources hunting for diamond mines all over the world. He never discovered one, and he ended his life destitute and depressed. Ironically the man who bought Hafed's farm made a discovery of his own. One day his camel stopped to drink from a brook on his property. As he rested on the camel, he noticed a sparkling light that glistened from the bottom of the creek. He climbed down and retrieved a glassy stone whose radiant brilliance was almost blinding. This gem was the first of many to be discovered. In fact, it led to the unearthing of the most famous diamond repository in history, the diamond mine of Golconda.

Although Hafed's story is extreme, many Christians make a similarly tragic oversight. They spend their lives on a journey searching for what they don't have rather than recognizing the abundant resources God has provided specifically for them. Some believers exhaust themselves attempting to become something God never intended them to be. They measure their value to him based on others' callings and how the Lord is using them. But when we look at others' abilities, our deficiencies become magnified in our mind. In coveting the spiritual accolades and accomplishments of others, we begin to feel useless and unimportant. If we fail to fulfill God's will for us because we feel ill equipped and insignificant, we forfeit God's best for us and fail to ever discover our full potential in Christ.

If you've ever struggled with feeling inadequate for God's will, as you "consider your calling" be encouraged by the biblical example of those God has used in the past. "Not many were wise from a human perspective, not many powerful, not many of noble birth" (1 Cor 1:26). God does not expect all of his people to be supremely talented. Instead, by his grace we are all spiritually gifted.

Scripture teaches us that God has given us spiritual gifts to accomplish his will. Individually our gifts enable us to fulfill his plan for our lives. Collectively our gifts enable God's people to achieve his mission. Yet many people live their whole lives without ever identifying their gifts or considering how their gifts should shape their calling. Scripture provides us with the necessary insight to understand spiritual gifts and how they are intended to operate. The Bible also helps us to discern our own giftedness in order to clarify our calling as we recognize how God has equipped us for his service.

1 Corinthians 12 (selected verses): [1]Now concerning spiritual gifts: brothers and sisters, I do not want you to be unaware. . . .

[4]Now there are different gifts, but the same Spirit. [5]There are different ministries, but the same Lord. [6]And there are different activities, but the same God produces each gift in each person. [7]A manifestation of the Spirit is given to each

person for the common good . . . [11]One and the same Spirit is active in all these, distributing to each person as he wills.

[12]For just as the body is one and has many parts, and all the parts of that body, though many, are one body—so also is Christ. . . . [18]But as it is, God has arranged each one of the parts in the body just as he wanted.

Romans 12:4–6: [4]Now as we have many parts in one body, and all the parts do not have the same function, [5]in the same way we who are many are one body in Christ and individually members of one another. [6]According to the grace given to us, we have different gifts.

1 Peter 4:10–11: [10]Just as each one has received a gift, use it to serve others, as good stewards of the varied grace of God. [11]If anyone speaks, let it be as one who speaks God's words; if anyone serves, let it be from the strength God provides, so that God may be glorified through Jesus Christ in everything. To him be the glory and the power forever and ever. Amen.

The God of Spiritual Gifts

Spiritual gifts are theological by nature. Their essence reflects fundamental truths about God. As the apostle Paul informs believers, there are "different gifts . . . different ministries . . . (and) different activities." But the basis for the various gifts and their uses is "the same Spirit . . . the same Lord [Jesus] . . . [and] the same God [the Father]" (1 Cor 12:4–6). The reference to the Trinity in this passage is essential for understanding spiritual gifts.

These verses of Scripture equate the Father, the Son, and the Spirit, affirming the triune God. Similarly, the three members of the Trinity are equated in other biblical passages through similar parallel phrasing (see 2 Cor 13:13; Matt 28:19). Although the persons of the Trinity are all equal in essence, they also perform specific roles. For instance, Scripture affirms the Father as the architect of redemption, the author of redemptive history. The Son's substitutionary and sacrificial death identifies him as the atonement of redemption. And our salvation is personally received, applied, and sealed by the Spirit, the agent of redemption (Eph 1:3–14). In the same way that there are distinct members of the Godhead, who are equal in nature and have particular functions, the members of Christ's body are all individual persons, equal in nature, who serve according to their designated responsibilities. In other words, spiritual gifts operate with unity and diversity, reflecting the very God who is their source and standard.

This means that spiritual gifts are also theological in function. Their definition and description ground them in God's power and plan. As it relates to God's power, our gifts always function according to "the strength God provides" (1 Pet 4:11). In relation to his plan, he has designed and distributed spiritual gifts to accomplish his purposes as we work together, functioning as his body (Rom 12:4–5). Therefore, our gifts reveal his will and reflect his ways by providing insight into his desires for our lives, leading us to serve him accordingly. The God of spiritual gifts—his unity, diversity, and functionality—is the basis for our understanding of our own giftedness and how he intends for us to use our gifts.

The Granting of Spiritual Gifts

Another important aspect concerning spiritual gifts is their allocation. Our spiritual gifts are not something that we are born possessing. In this way, they differ from natural talents that are abilities, skills, or capacities that we have independent of our relationship with Jesus. Talented singers, athletes, or artists may or may not be Christians. And although many Christians use their natural talents in service to the Lord, these are not the same as spiritual gifts. The granting of spiritual gifts, when and how we receive them, can help us to understand our giftedness and its role in accomplishing God's will for our lives.

Our spiritual gifts are not received at our physical conception, but at our spiritual conversion. When we trust Jesus Christ as our Lord and Savior, we receive the Holy Spirit who dwells within us (1 Cor 6:19; Eph 1:13–14). As he takes up residence in our lives, he distributes at least one spiritual gift to every believer (1 Pet 4:10; 1 Cor 12:6–7). This means that our spiritual gifts are not earned or manufactured. They cannot be sought or attained. They are "gifts" from God (Rom 12:6).[1] God distributes spiritual gifts to individuals according to his will (1 Cor 12:11). This means that while there may be gifts that are more prominent and public, no spiritual gift can be elevated over another. Each member of Christ's body plays a unique and critical role according to his or her giftedness (1 Cor 12:20–22), functioning as a supporting part that enables the body to mature and grow into the fullness of Christ (Eph 4:15–16).

Your gift(s) are given to you by God to accomplish his will for your life. The spiritual gifts you possess are by design and are for a purpose. Although you cannot earn or manufacture spiritual gifts, you can develop the ones you've been given. Oftentimes they complement your natural talents and perfectly equip you to accomplish God's will for your life. The reality of your giftedness also means

---

[1] The root word of the term that is often translated as "gifts" (charisma) means "grace" (charis). This further affirms the benevolent nature of spiritual gifts and our inability to earn or manufacture them.

that your role within the body of Christ, both global and local, is an essential aspect of fulfilling his plan for you.

The Goal of Spiritual Gifts

Since our spiritual gifts are given to us by God according to his specific plan for our lives, it is easy to consider them from an individual perspective. But even though we personally receive and use our gifts, they obviously do not function in isolation. Our gifts are used to influence others around us as we live to honor Christ. By nature, spiritual gifts are designed and intended to function for the benefit of others and "the common good" (1 Cor 12:7). Collectively our gifts serve a specific purpose within the body of Christ that allows it to function according to God's design (vv. 12, 18). Therefore, our gifts are actually a responsibility that God has entrusted to us as members of his family (Rom 12:4–5).

In addition to functioning for the common good, our gifts are meant to function for Christ's glory. Although some churches focus on the individuals who have certain gifts, particularly those that seem to be more prominent or public in nature, spiritual gifts are never intended to bestow honor on the person using them. Since gifts are not earned or manufactured, there is no room for boasting. The equal value of the various spiritual gifts also removes any basis for individual accolades or admiration.

The nature of spiritual gifts inherently deflects glory from the gift or the individual to the One who is the source and strength of our giftedness. All of the biblical passages that speak to spiritual gifts centralize the focus on God rather than the individual, on Christ rather than his servant. Therefore, our gifts must be used "so that God may be glorified through Jesus Christ in everything. To him be the glory and the power forever and ever" (1 Pet 4:11). This means that our spiritual gifts must be embraced with thanksgiving; they must be employed with modesty; they must be enjoyed with Christ-honoring praise.

Although it is tempting to focus on our gifts as personal abilities to help us achieve God's will for our individual lives, we must be careful not to approach them as a means of personal gain. They do guide us to discern God's will and equip us to fulfill it, but we also have to remember that God intends for them to serve a purpose beyond ourselves. Your spiritual gifts are meant to impact the lives of others, both individually and corporately within the body of Christ. We must also remember that our gifts are not designed to call attention to ourselves and our abilities, but to bring glory to the One who has gifted us as we honor our Savior, Jesus Christ. As you devote yourself to developing and using your spiritual gifts, serve the Lord and others with humility and gratitude, being mindful of God's undeserved grace and giftedness (1 Pet 4:10).

Living It Out

Many believers have never seriously considered their spiritual gifts. But think about it: if God has gifted us for a specific purpose and equipped us to serve in a particular role, then apart from recognizing and using those spiritual gifts, it will be next to impossible to fulfill God's will for us. It is critical for us to discern our gifts and consider the most effective and efficient ways to use them for Christ.

Explore Your Gifts. God has entrusted you as a believer with spiritual gifts as part of his plan for your life. This means that you have a responsibility to explore your gifts, to identify them, and to determine how the Lord wants you to use them. The scriptural lists of spiritual gifts (1 Cor 12:8–10; Rom 12:6–8) are not intended to be exhaustive, but they indicate the types of gifts with which God equips us for his service. They might be categorized as speaking gifts (1 Pet 4:11), such as preaching and teaching; serving gifts (1 Pet 4:11), such as leading, giving, and mercy; and sign gifts (1 Cor 12:9–10), such as healing and miracles.[2]

As you explore the biblical lists of gifts, consider ways to assess your giftedness. Spiritual gifts tests/inventories, available online or through your church, can be beneficial guides in determining how God has equipped you for his service. Fellow believers and church leaders can also provide helpful observations and insights. Through your involvement in the local church, others have the opportunity to recognize your spiritual abilities and gifts.

Perhaps the best way to explore your gifts is to begin serving according to your interests, abilities, and desires. The spiritual passions that motivate you, the opportunities that become available, the ministries that you are suited for, and the skills you possess—all can point to or reveal your gifts. Remember, your natural talents and interests will complement your spiritual gifts and abilities. As you make yourself available to the Lord, involve yourself in the ministries of your local church and trust him as you step into unfamiliar opportunities, God will confirm your giftedness. His affirmation will include a sense of unparalleled fulfillment, spiritual fruit evident in yourself and in those you serve, and a desire to grow in a particular capacity.

Exercise Your Gifts. Fulfilling God's will for your life involves using the gifts he has entrusted to you. As you recognize your gifts, you'll want to strengthen and develop them. Although we cannot manufacture spiritual gifts, like anything else, by actively using

---

[2] Sign gifts have always been intended as a visible and tangible testimony that validates and verifies the gospel (Luke 9:1–6; Acts 4:5–12). As a result, they primarily function in missional and evangelistic contexts, function according to God's intention and empowerment, and testify to his grace for his glory (Heb 2:3–4).

them, we become more proficient with them. As we become more familiar with our ministry for the Lord, both inside and outside the local church, we will also grow more comfortable with our gifts. There are also some basic principles that can help us strengthen our understanding and use of them.

Although you receive your spiritual gifts at conversion, some gifts are developed through time and experience. Let's say you have the spiritual gift of teaching. But explaining and expounding God's Word requires a familiarity with Scripture that comes only through diligent study. You may recognize the gift prior to your ability or opportunity to use it. Or through your own maturing process, you might gradually discern the gift. Either way, when you possess spiritual gifts that require growth and development, your responsibility does not begin when opportunity arises. You must devote yourself to strengthening your spiritual abilities, to be ready to use them. Through your faithful preparation, God will provide the perfect opportunity at the proper time for you to use your gifts.

In addition, some gifts might be seasonal. Depending on where you are along God's path for you, there might be a particular gift that is immediately active and functional. At other times, God may desire to expand your ministry. During these seasons, you still possess your gifts, but there might be other needs in the body that a particular gift is perfectly suited to meet. As you use previously unforeseen gifts according to the available opportunities, continue to look for ways to grow in every aspect of your giftedness. It is not uncommon for new seasonal gifts to develop only to culminate in full bloom at some later time when all of the elements combine and your gifts function together.

God is grooming you and growing your gifts to fulfill his plan. Initially you might feel awkward serving according to your newly discovered giftedness. Your spiritual gifts might require you to stretch past what feels comfortable. Or they might shoulder you with responsibilities you do not feel prepared to handle. But God's plan for your life will always lead you beyond where you can journey on your own. By faith, exercise your gifts, knowing that he has perfectly equipped you to accomplish everything he has called you to do!

Employ Your Gifts. When you recognize your giftedness, you cannot allow your gifts to remain dormant. God's will for you involves you serving according to your giftedness. When we don't discern our gifts, we become spiritually stifled. When we recognize our gifts but don't use them, we become spiritually stagnant. Our hearts can become frustrated because we are not functioning according to God's design. We can grow discouraged because we do not feel useful for the Lord. But when we exercise and employ our gifts, we will sense God's presence and power in our lives. His joy and fulfillment will flood our hearts. We will see his hand at work, enabling us to become more than we ever imagined and equipping us to accomplish more than we could have ever envisioned.

Therefore, as you discern your gifts, you should devote yourself to using them. Scripture instructs us, "as each one has received a gift, use it to serve others, as good stewards" of the gifts God has entrusted (1 Pet 4:10). In other words, we have a spiritual responsibility to invest our gifts in the lives of others by being actively involved among God's people. The biblical metaphor of the church as a body teaches us that we all have a specific role to play and function to perform (1 Cor 12:14–22). Our spiritual gifts identify us metaphorically as an eye or an ear, a hand or a foot. As such, our function is indispensable to the body. The particular part does not serve itself, but the body as a whole.

This means that for the body of Christ to mature we must employ our gifts to serve others. Individually, as we minister to others, we grow in our faith and we also encourage them to grow. Collectively, as each of us uses our gifts to serve others, the church develops "until we all reach unity in the faith and in the knowledge of God's Son, growing into maturity with a stature measured by Christ's fullness" (Eph 4:13). When we serve according to our giftedness, it "promotes the growth of the body for building up itself in love by the proper working of each individual part" (Eph 4:16). Therefore, we must look for opportunities to serve the Lord and his people, to accomplish God's will for our lives and the life of his church.

It is easy for us to recognize what we enjoy and the types of ministries we gravitate toward, but, thinking realistically, we may find ourselves serving according to our preferences rather than our giftedness. When this happens, we displace someone else who may be more suited to serve in the capacity we are occupying. We also misplace our own giftedness by serving in a way that may not maximize our usefulness for the Lord. This cripples the body of Christ and hinders our ability to fulfill our calling. So it's crucial for you to explore, exercise, and employ your gifts to determine how God has equipped you to best discern the plan he has designed for you.

It is important to note that there are Christian responsibilities that are expectations for all believers regardless of one's gifts. For instance, even if you are not spiritually gifted for service, giving, or mercy (Rom 12:7), you are not exempt from these foundational acts of Christian obedience. We are all expected to serve one another in love (Gal 5:13), to give generously (2 Cor 9:7), and to show mercy to others (Mic 6:8). While we focus on our gifts, we cannot neglect our spiritual responsibilities as devoted disciples of Christ. It is through our faithfulness to God's Word that our gifts will become evident, will develop, and will be effective for the Lord.

65

Jesus told the parable about a master who entrusted his servants with certain possessions while he was away (Matt 25:14–30). Some servants used their gifts effectively, investing their gifts and multiplying them. These servants were active with their gifts, and by faith they performed the master's work and accomplished his will. But one of the servants was afraid of failure. Because of his fear, he buried his talent. Although he remained active, he never used his gift to produce any fruit for his master's kingdom. When the master returned, those who had used their gifts were commended as "faithful" for a job "well done." The one who buried his gift was rebuked as "lazy" and proved to be an unworthy servant.

Similarly, God has entrusted each of us with gifts and opportunities. When we fail to use our gifts, we ultimately fail to please our Master. But when we serve him with all that he has entrusted to us, devoting ourselves fully to his kingdom by actively investing in others, we will be commended by him with the highest honor, "Well done, good and faithful servant!" (Matt 25:23).

PART III

ABIDING IN CHRIST

H ave you ever found yourself standing in the middle of your kitchen and wondering why you came in there in the first place? Not long ago, I was sitting in our den when Cassie, our youngest daughter, asked me if she could have a bowl of grapes for a snack. When I got up to get them, I noticed that our dog, Copper, needed to go out. So after I opened the back door for him, I walked into the kitchen and noticed some dirty dishes begging for attention. So I stopped to rinse them off and place them in the dishwasher. By this time, Copper was scratching at the back door. After letting him back inside, I paused and thought, "What was it I came in here to get?" When I couldn't immediately remember, I opened the refrigerator, grabbed a soda, and returned to my chair in the den. As soon as I sat down, Cassie impatiently questioned me from the couch, "Daddy, where are my grapes?!" All I could do was put my head down and laugh as I scurried back to the kitchen. I had completely forgotten the reason I had gotten up in the first place.

In the same way, as Christians many times we can get busy doing things for God. Good things, godly things. But in the midst of our busyness for him, we can lose sight of the primary purpose we are striving to achieve. God's will for our lives and his calling share an ultimate goal—knowing him. Everything we are called to do is meant to draw us into a deeper relationship with Christ, that we may know him in a more personal way, that we might "abide" in him.

This is why near the conclusion of his earthly ministry Jesus encouraged his disciples, using the image of fruit (grapes) that abides in the vine. "As the Father has loved me, so have I loved you. Abide in my love. If you keep my commandments, you will abide in my love, just as I have kept my Father's commandments and abide in his love. These things I have spoken to you, that my joy may be in you, and that your joy may be full" (John 15:9–11 ESV). This intimate knowledge and ongoing relationship with Christ became Paul's ambition as well. After reviewing his earthly résumé and considering all that he had accomplished for God, he summarized his ultimate purpose, "My goal is to know him" (Phil 3:10).

God has always desired an intimate relationship with his people. In the Old Testament, Israel continually strayed from God. They attempted to maintain his rules and guidelines, but even when they obeyed his commands it was not from the heart. Their obedience came from a sense of obligation and duty. And when they experienced success in life, they began to focus more on their accomplishments and achieving worldly fame. Accumulating riches and gaining notoriety subtly became their goals; as a result, these things became their gods. They lost sight of their purpose. They had essentially forgotten the grapes and abiding in the vine. So God sent the prophet Jeremiah to deliver his message for them. His message for his people is still the same today: knowing God should always be our ultimate goal, the one thing we can never forget. This passage reveals several truths that can help us maintain our focus on knowing God as we fulfill his will for our lives.

Jeremiah 9:23–24: [23]This is what the Lord says: The wise person should not boast in his wisdom; the strong should not boast in his strength; the wealthy should not boast in his wealth. [24]But the one who boasts should boast in this: that he understands and knows me—that I am the LORD, showing faithful love, justice, and righteousness on the earth, for I delight in these things. This is the LORD's declaration.

Knowing God Should Be Our Consuming Passion

The Lord begins his admonition for them by elevating their personal relationship with him above everything else. These two verses use the term *boast* several times to describe where we find our confidence. So he doesn't indict wisdom or riches or strength, but he cautions us not to find our security in them. When these things become our goal, we "boast" in them by placing our confidence and trust in them. The same things that distracted Israel from their ultimate goal of knowing God are often the obstacles that divert our attention away from growing in our relationship with him.

If knowing God is going to be our motivating passion, *we can't be consumed with wisdom.* We live in an information age. Knowledge and facts are readily accessible through unlimited resources. It's easy to mistake understanding or intelligence for wisdom and devote ourselves to the goal of acquiring knowledge. But earthly wisdom works against a deeper understanding of God.

The two are in opposition to each other (Jas 3:13–18). Where the world's wisdom says, "eyes on the prize" and "by any means necessary," God says, "Do nothing out of selfish ambition or conceit, but in humility consider others as more important than yourselves. Everyone should look out not only for his own interests, but also for the interests of others" (Phil 2:3–4). When the world's wisdom says, "Revenge is sweet," God says, "Bless those who persecute you; bless and do not curse," and "Do not repay anyone evil for

69

evil" (Rom 12:14, 17). God's ways are not the ways of the world (Isa 55:8–9). He has actually chosen to work through the simple things of this life to confuse the wise and undermine the wisdom of this world (1 Cor 1:21–25). We recognize this in the ultimate example of Christ, who humbled himself in order to be exalted, who suffered as guilty even though he was innocent, and who died on the cross that he might defeat death and grant us life. True understanding in this life is found through knowing God.

He also instructs us that *we can't be consumed with works.* These days, ability and achievement are elevated as the ultimate prize. Success is often measured by someone's physical strength or positional status. People devote their entire lives to accomplishing worldly goals, only to be disappointed by failure or the lack of genuine satisfaction when they are attained. But earthly abilities and achievements are temporary, short-lived, and empty pursuits.

Those things of eternal value are accomplished, "not by strength or by might, but by my Spirit says the LORD" (Zech 4:6). This is why Jesus taught us, "You can do nothing without me" (John 15:5), and yet, with Christ, there's nothing in his strength that we can't do (Phil 4:13). This is why God told Paul, "My grace is sufficient for you, for my power is perfected in weakness," which led the apostle to conclude, "I will most gladly boast all the more about my weaknesses, so that Christ's power may reside in me. . . . For when I am weak, then I am strong" (2 Cor 12:9–10). Therefore, when we are consumed with knowing God, we cannot focus on what we can or cannot do. We also must be careful not to evaluate our own spiritual progress by what we have done for him. Instead, we should always be focused on what he, in Christ, has done for us.

Lastly, God cautioned us that *we can't be consumed with wealth.* Material possessions, especially in the United States, are often the measure of success. The size of one's bank accounts, the price of one's cars, or ownership of the latest gadget—all are used to evaluate a person's worth. But in God's economy, earthly possessions are temporary and superficial. Money is not intrinsically sinful, but the pursuit of it is deadly. The Bible cautions us, "But those who want to be rich fall into temptation, a trap, and many foolish and harmful desires, which plunge people into ruin and destruction. For the love of money is a root of all kinds of evil, and by craving it, some have wandered away from the faith and pierced themselves with many griefs" (1 Tim 6:9–10). Jesus taught that serving God and money simultaneously is impossible (Matt 6:24), because what we value reveals the true passions of our hearts (Matt 6:21).

Therefore, we are called to store up for ourselves "treasures in heaven" (Matt 6:19–20). We can use our earthly wealth to invest in kingdom purposes. As Scripture teaches us,

> Instruct those who are rich in the present age not to be arrogant or to set their hope on the uncertainty of wealth, but on God, who richly provides us with all things to enjoy. Instruct them to do what is good, to be rich in good works, to be generous and willing to share, storing up treasure for themselves as a good foundation for the coming age, so that they may take hold of what is truly life. (1 Tim 6:17–19)

So acquiring wealth should never be our ultimate goal, but knowing God, while using wealth to help others come to know him, should be our consuming passion.

These three common obstacles—wisdom, works, and wealth—serve as a comprehensive summary of what life is apart from Christ. Without him, life consists of what we know, what we can do, and what we have. But, in reflecting on his impressive earthly résumé, Paul came to the conclusion, "I also consider everything to be a loss in view of the surpassing value of knowing Christ Jesus my Lord. Because of him I have suffered the loss of all things and consider them as dung, so that I may gain Christ" (Phil 3:8).

Like Paul, knowing Christ must become our consuming passion. This means that Jesus cannot be merely an addition to our life; he must be the addiction of our life! We should want to get alone with him, check on his updated status, and risk everything by gambling on him. Nothing else compares with Christ; therefore, we should not let anything else compete with Christ for our heart's supreme devotion.

Knowing God Achieves Our Created Purpose

Instead of finding our hope in our wisdom, works, and wealth, God tells us that the one source of confidence should be "that he understands and knows me" (Jer 9:24). The magnitude of this statement is beyond belief and defies description. How is it that we, as created beings, can know and understand, in a real and personal way, God our Creator?! Yet he says it's possible. That's because of how and why he created us.

God did not create us because he was bored or lonely. He didn't create us to show off. God created us for a personal relationship with him. It's seen in the exclusive nature we bear as people. The Bible records our uniqueness in the creation account, where God declared, "Let us make man in our image, according to our likeness. . . . So God created man in his own image; he created him in the image of God; he created them male and female" (Gen 1:26–27).

Being created in God's image includes having a unique intellectual capacity, as we have the potential for creative and complex thoughts that are reflective of God and surpass that of other created beings. We also possess a moral capacity that includes a conscience and an innate sense of right and wrong. But the primary aspect of God's image is a relational capacity that we possess. When he declared, "Let *us* make man in *our* image," the plural terms imply the triune nature of God in the persons of the Father, the Son, and the Holy Spirit. But it also indicates the relational intimacy they share as One and the potential for a relationship with God that we possess by design.

✱Adam and Eve were created for fellowship with God, but when they sinned in the Garden humanity's relationship with God was broken. As a result, we still possess the relational capacity, but it is damaged by sin's consequences, and our sinful nature prevents us from the ability to initiate or restore our relationship with him. This leaves us in a helpless position, but, because of God's grace, it is not a hopeless position. God has taken the necessary steps to reconcile our relationship with him.

First, *he has displayed his power.* God has revealed himself to us through creation. The beauty of a sunrise, the massive height and breadth of the mountains, the depths of the ocean, and the vastness of the universe, combined with the intricate design of it all—this is God's megaphone that pronounces his existence. This is why the psalmist said, "The heavens declare the glory of God, and the expanse proclaims the work of his hands (Ps 19:1). Likewise, Paul said, "For his invisible attributes, that is, his eternal power and divine nature, have been clearly seen since the creation of the world, being understood through what he has made" (Rom 1:20). But the knowledge available through creation about God is broad and nonspecific. It allows us to know that God is real, but it does not tell us what God is really like.

Therefore, in addition to this general revelation, *he has disclosed his person.* Through his Word, the written word of Scripture and the living word of Jesus Christ, God has revealed the more personal attributes of his nature. Scripture is the Word of God (Heb 4:12), and through divine inspiration he discloses his personal characteristics to us (2 Tim 3:16). Jesus is the eternal Word of God who became man and physically revealed God to us (John 1:1, 14, 18). He made what was otherwise invisible, visible (Col 1:15), and the fullness of God dwelt in him in bodily form (Col 2:9). Since Jesus is "the radiance of God's glory and the exact expression of his nature" (Heb 1:3), we can know the personal attributes of God as they are embodied and revealed through the person of Jesus Christ.

Although God has revealed himself to us, our relational capacity is still in need of restoration for us to reconcile our relationship with God. Therefore, through Christ, *God has delivered his people.* Jesus died on the cross as a substitute for our sin so that he might bring us back to God (Col 1:20; 1 Pet 3:18). His sacrifice purchased our salvation, gives us new life, rescues us from death, delivers us into his kingdom, and forgives us of our sins (Col 1:13–14). Our salvation, often referred to as eternal life, is defined by Jesus as the restored relationship we have with God through a personal knowledge of Christ (John 17:3).

God created us for a personal relationship with him. Despite our sin, and because of his great mercy and love, God has redeemed us from sin, to reconcile, or repair, our relationship. Therefore, through Christ, we can achieve our created purpose of knowing God.

Knowing God Requires Our Constant Pursuit

Although God has made it possible for us to know him, our relationship with him does not simply involve an introduction to him. To understand and know him becomes a lifelong journey into the unfathomable depths of the majestic beauty and infinite wisdom of "the knowledge of God" (Rom 11:33). But how do we explore and experience more of God? How does our relationship with him progress?

✱ To grow in our knowledge of God, *we must progress beyond spiritual infancy*. God's challenge to understand and know him is followed by his personal declaration, "I am the LORD, showing faithful love, justice, and righteousness on the earth" (Jer 9:24). The first level of our knowledge of God is a truth-based, factual understanding of him. He is a loving, just, and righteous God. From God's Word we read of these attributes, and our affections are stimulated and deepened. As we learn more about him, we are attracted to his infinite glory and majestic nature. We become spiritually enamored and desire a deeper knowledge of him. This personal understanding and informative knowledge is only the initial stage of our relational growth.

✱ In addition, *we must proceed into spiritual intimacy*. God does not merely identify his characteristics in a static fashion. He states, "I am the LORD who, *showing* faithful love, justice, and righteousness on the earth" (v. 24, italics mine). This does not mean he merely displays or exhibits these attributes. They are extended to his people, and we are able to experience them. This type of experiential knowledge goes deeper than the empirical knowledge that consists of factual truths.

For example, it's one thing to acknowledge that God is merciful, but it's much more personal when we experience his mercy. Similarly, to know that the Lord is the God of all comfort is encouraging, but when we experience that comfort in the loss of a loved one, our understanding of God goes so much deeper. Likewise, to know that God is the ultimate provider is a truth we can claim, but to trust him and experience his provision in financial hardship allows us to know him in a more immediate and tangible way.

Every aspect of our lives should seek to experience the Lord in these personal ways. The more factual truths we learn about God, the more we will be able to recognize his work in our lives. As a result, we can actively experience his attributes and enjoy a stronger and more personal relationship with him. When we begin to experience these truths, we could be satisfied with this level of knowledge, but he desires an even deeper level.

In addition to spiritual infancy and intimacy, *we must pursue him with spiritual intensity*. The final phrase in these verses tells us that the Lord exercises his attributes "on the earth, for I delight in these things" (v. 24). At first glance, it appears that God is interested in exhibiting his greatness to bring himself pleasure. Although he certainly does delight in exercising his goodness, his attributes are not simply extended in a general, or spiritual, manner. His characteristics are active "on the earth" through his people. And when we exhibit his attributes, he takes great delight in their expression.

This is the deepest level of knowing God that we must constantly pursue—the embodied knowledge of who he is as displayed through our lives. Consider these examples: I learn and believe that God is merciful; when I sin, through faith and repentance I experience that mercy. Then, when someone mistreats me, I take my knowledge of God and put it into action by extending mercy to that person. Or I believe that God provides, and by faith I trust him to meet my needs. As he does and I encounter others who are in need, I give and support them as God extends his provision through me. In other words, our knowledge of God grows (1) from being the truths that we affirm (2) to being that which we personally experience as God extends himself to us (3) to becoming ultimately what God accomplishes through us!

As we embody the character of God that we have personally experienced, the Lord will work through us to accomplish his will.

When we see him actively working, not only in but through our lives, our knowledge of him will intensify and joy will flood our hearts as he delights in us. To elevate knowing him as our highest priority in order to achieve our created purpose will require our constant pursuit. And it begins with a simple prayer, asking God to fulfill his historic promise to his people in our lives today, "I will give them a heart to know me, that I am the LORD" (Jer 24:7).

Looking Ahead

If knowing God in a more personal and intimate way is going to become our driving motivation in life, we must devote ourselves to the spiritual disciplines that position us to "grow in the grace and knowledge of our Lord and Savior Jesus Christ" (2 Pet 3:18). God has provided two primary means by which we can experience his presence and transforming power in our lives. Prayer and God's Word grant us access to his grace to grow in our relationship with him. The chapters in this section will help you understand why these two spiritual disciplines are so vital to your spiritual journey and will teach you how to integrate them into your life.

CHAPTER 5

We Can Approach His Throne

A familiar story recounts how a remote African village of new believers maintained their vibrant faith. Early on in their Christian walk, they recognized the fundamental importance of prayer. To encourage personal devotion, each member of the community established a place for personal retreat to spend time alone with God. Based on the location of their village, the young Christians had to carve their own paths through the brush to reach their personal place. Talk about a commitment to pray, they were all in!

For these young Christians, like many of us, there were times when they struggled to pray consistently and regularly. Unlike us, however, it did not remain a secret. Their lack of devotion became obvious to their brothers and sisters in Christ because grass grew over their paths. Out of genuine concern for one another, and in an effort to hold the community accountable, they developed a loving way to prompt one another to renew their commitment to pray. They would simply observe, "Friend, there's grass on your path."

If we could observe one another's prayer life today, I wonder how many of us would be guilty of an overgrown path. When we consider making progress in prayer, this is not the type of "growth" God desires! But, sadly, it is far too common. As Christians, we are often guilty of giving "lip service" to prayer while failing to practice lip service in prayer. But prayer is a fundamental discipline of the Christian life that we cannot live without. It is the spiritual avenue God has provided for us to encounter his presence and fellowship with him. Yet we continually fail to take advantage of this divine privilege. When we do, we forfeit God's blessings in our lives and the precious time of personal communion with our Savior. This neglect also prevents us from experiencing the powerful effect prayer has on our hearts that ultimately equips us to accomplish his will for our lives.

In Luke 18, Jesus emphasized the importance and essential nature of prayer by telling his disciples a parable about a widow. Simply defined, a parable is an earthly story with a heavenly meaning. It uses the familiar to explain the unfamiliar. Sometimes the meaning of parables is left for us to discern. However, in some cases, like this one, Jesus explains or explicitly states the point of his parable. Prayer is essential. Without it, we will lose heart and give up. But through prayer, God will sustain us and empower us to live victoriously in Christ. Our prayers, however, cannot simply be casual, halfhearted acknowledgments of God's goodness. Jesus's parable teaches us that we must be desperate in prayer as we approach his throne.

Luke 18:1–8: [1]Now he told them a parable on the need for them to pray always and not give up. [2]"There was a judge in a certain town who didn't fear God or respect people. [3]And a widow in that town kept coming to him, saying, 'Give me justice against my adversary.'

[4]"For a while he was unwilling, but later he said to himself, 'Even though I don't fear God or respect people, [5]yet because this widow keeps pestering me, I will give her

justice, so that she doesn't wear me out by her persistent coming.'"

[6]Then the Lord said, "Listen to what the unjust judge says. [7]Will not God grant justice to his elect who cry out to him day and night? Will he delay helping them? [8]I tell you that he will swiftly grant them justice. Nevertheless, when the Son of Man comes, will he find faith on earth?"

When Jesus told this parable he was speaking of the end times when sin, worldliness, and lostness would be rampant. His warning for the disciples was that apart from prayer they would not be able to endure. Prayer would be the necessary lifeline that would sustain them. Our current culture reflects these same characteristics, and we all know that "desperate times call for desperate measures." Like the disciples, we must completely rely on God through prayer. Jesus's parable teaches us three truths that will fuel our prayer life.

Desperate Prayer Is Dictated by Our Futility

Jesus's parable about the persistent widow was intended to draw an obvious comparison to his listeners (and to us as readers). In the first-century culture, a childless widow was completely helpless. As a woman, her positional status in society did not allow her to provide for herself. And as a widow, she also had no one to provide for her. She had no family, no representation, and no support. She was not only helpless; she was hopeless. The widow was completely at the mercy of the judge.

Although our domestic situations may not parallel the widow's, our spiritual condition leaves us just as helpless and hopeless. We cannot do anything to earn God's favor or to deserve his kindness. And we do not have the ability or the means to overcome the world on our own. In addition, like the widow, we can't depend on anyone else to do it for us. Our parents, our families, our friends—none of them can provide what we need to have a relationship with God and to offer hope for this life. We are entirely dependent on his mercy.

Until we understand the critical nature of our situations, we will not recognize the need for desperate prayer. In telling this parable, Jesus was helping us to appreciate just how bleak our situation is apart from God's help. Too many times, we fail to see the futility of our best efforts, our renewed commitments, and our sincere intentions. But Jesus told the parable for the very purpose of teaching us that apart from prayer we might as well give up (v. 1). In this way, we are just like the hopeless widow.

However, unlike us, the widow did not have to be convinced. She knew that she did not stand a chance left to her own efforts and resources. The desperate nature of her appeals reveals her clear understanding. But her desperation wasn't based solely on her lack of ability; it was also due to the strength of her adversary (v. 3). Like the widow, we have an enemy, Satan, who is prowling around like a roaring lion wanting to devour us (1 Pet 5:8). Jesus warned that he comes "to steal and kill and destroy" (John 10:10). With his spiritual forces of darkness, he is waging war against us (Eph 6:11–12). He appeals to our sinful desires and works through a corrupt world to form a potent attack from both directions, internal and external, in an effort to defeat us.

Satan's strength, compounded by our weakness, leaves us desperate for help. We, like the widow, must appeal to God for "justice" (vv. 3, 5, 7), which he, in his mercy, grants us in Christ. Jesus is our advocate (1 John 2:1) who lives to make intercession on our behalf (Heb 7:25). Through his sacrifice on the cross, God extends to us the mercy we desperately need. Therefore, through faith in Christ's victory, we can overcome the world and the power of the enemy (John 16:33; 1 John 5:4).

The desperation of our prayers will directly correspond with our willingness to recognize the futility of our condition apart from Christ. Our lack of prayer demonstrates a belief, whether we admit it or not, that we don't think we need God's help. Not to pray is ultimately a declaration of prideful independence. It is the most arrogant way to say to God, "I don't need you. I've got this. I can do it on my own." But when we have an accurate view of our condition, we will appeal to God in desperate prayer.

Sometimes God uses difficult situations to teach us how to depend on him through prayer. Other times we can recognize our need for prayer through some of the typical symptoms of prayerlessness: discouragement, anxiety, frustration, or restlessness. But ultimately our need for prayer is not determined by our difficult circumstances or emotional feelings. Desperate prayer stems from the futility of our condition and the recognition of our critical need for God's continual love, support, mercy, and strength.

Desperate Prayer Is Demonstrated by Our Fervency

The parable of the widow does not teach us merely why our prayer life is essential; it teaches us what our prayer life should look like. Jesus describes the persistence of the widow to demonstrate the determination and diligence with which we ought to pray. Consider how Jesus portrays the widow's constant appeals. Describing her ongoing passion and persistence, he tells us that she "kept coming" to the judge (v. 3). The unrighteous judge laments the wearying effects of her bombarding pleas for justice, concluding, she will "wear me out with her persistent coming" (v. 5). The same heartfelt fervency the widow pleaded with is meant to provide the example for our prayer lives. Jesus told the parable so that his disciples would learn to "pray always" (v. 1) as those who "cry out" to the Lord "day and night" (v. 7). Desperate prayer is demonstrated by our passionate and persistent pleas to the Lord.

Sadly, our prayer lives often drift in the opposite direction. Rather than being persistent, we are predictably inconsistent. In contrast, Scripture depicts prayer with a consistency and intensity that God desires for our personal times of communion with him. For example, James 5:16 describes faithful prayers as powerful and effective. Paul prescribed unceasing prayer as a continual God-consciousness and awareness of his presence in our lives, coupled with an utter dependence on him (1 Thess 5:17). Likewise, he challenged the Ephesians to "pray at all times" with all types of prayers and with "all perseverance" (6:18). These verses all depict the fervency that should characterize our prayer life.

Although Jesus's parable about the widow accurately portrays this type of persistent prayer, Jesus himself provided the greatest real-life example of what our prayer lives should look like. Scripture records that Jesus "often withdrew to deserted places to pray" (Luke 5:16). He retreated to be alone with the Father and to focus exclusively on time with him. We also know that Jesus prioritized prayer by rising "very early in the morning, while it was still dark" to pray (Mark 1:35).

His persistence was seen not only in his regular times of prayer, but also in the extended time he spent in prayer. The Bible records that Jesus regularly, "spent all night in prayer to God" (Luke 6:12). Jesus was passionate and persistent in his prayer life, and on the night before he was crucified, when he was in anguish, "he prayed more fervently" (Luke 22:44). It's interesting: his disciples witnessed countless miracles, listened to him teach masterfully, watched him minister to others' needs with mercy and compassion, but they never once asked him to teach them to do any of these things. They did, however, request, "Lord, teach us to pray" (Luke 11:1).

His unwavering devotion to prayer piqued their curiosity, but it also reflected the immeasurable value Jesus placed on prayer. If Jesus, the Son of God, was so fervent in prayer, how much more should we be faithful to pray?! Yet we often treat prayer as a spare tire; it's there if we ever need it in times of trouble. But prayer ought not be our last resort; it should be our first priority. Our prayer life should be passionate and persistent. The fervency of our prayers will be evidenced by the frequency of our prayers. Like the widow, and ultimately like our Savior, we must be relentless in our prayers. We must be diligent and devoted to spending time with God.

Desperate Prayer Is Determined by Our Faith

Although the desperate nature of our prayers begins with the understanding of our helpless and hopeless condition, it is ultimately determined by our faith in God. Our confidence is not in the prayer itself, the words we express, or the passion with which we voice it, but in the Lord himself, in whose name we pray. Our devotion to prayer derives from the deep conviction that we believe in the Lord. We trust that God hears our prayers, that he has the power to answer our prayers, and that he always responds to our prayers in a way that is best for us. Our faith in God—who he is, what he has done, and what he can and will do—will determine the desperate nature of our prayers.

The parable Jesus told draws a comparison between us and the persistent widow. But it also portrays a stark contrast between the judge she appealed to and the God to whom we pray. Jesus described the judge as one who did not "respect people" (vv. 2, 4). This attitude reflects a cold and indifferent heart. This is why Jesus described the judge as "unjust" (v. 6). But God is the God of justice, and his heart is exactly the opposite of this. It is overflowing with love and compassion for people. He cares for our needs; he grieves when we make mistakes; he empathizes with us when we are hurting and heartbroken. His care and concern for us are so deep that he sent his Son to die as our substitute, to pay the price for our sins, and to secure our eternity with him! Because of this, we can have confidence to bring our cares and concerns to him, because he cares for us (1 Pet 5:7). Since he did not spare his own Son but willingly gave him up on our behalf, we can know that he will not withhold anything we need (Rom 8:32).

Jesus also described the judge as being annoyed by the widow, who viewed her as one who "keeps pestering me" and would wear him out (v. 5). He was exasperated by her neediness, and he eventually conceded by giving in to her persistent requests. But God does not have to be convinced or coerced to answer our prayers. He is eager to respond on our behalf. Jesus captured this assurance by referring to God's people as "his elect" (v. 7), those with whom he has a unique relationship with through Christ. His covenant and unfailing love pledges his certain and swift response on our behalf (vv. 7–8).

Jesus concluded the parable with an important question, "When the Son of Man comes, will he find faith on earth?" (v. 8). In anticipating his return, Jesus challenged his listeners to consider who will remain. Who will persevere through this life? It will be those who have continued to rely on him by "faith." His question subtly equates faith with prayer. According to Jesus, prayer is the tangible expression of our faith! Our prayers directly reflect our view of God and the depth of our trust in him.

Many times we approach prayer as though God is similar to the unrighteous judge, as though our desperate pleas will persuade God to act on our behalf. But prayer does not change God, and we would not want him to change. We are the ones who need his comforting mercy and grace. Prayer changes us. When we come to God in prayer, it is similar to throwing an anchor from a boat. When it grabs hold of the shore and we pull on the rope, the shore does not come closer to us, but we are drawn closer to the shore. Prayer is the anchor that draws us closer to God, conforms our heart to his, and secures our confidence in him. And our faithfulness to pray, to cast our cares on him, will be determined by our faith.

Living It Out

We all know that prayer is foundational for our spiritual walk and daily lives. Yet when it comes to maintaining a consistent prayer life, we struggle. Some of our challenges can be resolved by designing an approach based on biblical principles that will guide our times with the Lord. Here are two practical steps that you can use to enhance your prayer life.

Step 1: Formulate a Prayer Strategy. Many of us would like to pray more, but we simply don't know how. There aren't magic words, certain phrases, or even a specific voice we are supposed to use. It should come from the heart and, in many ways, should be a simple conversation between God and us. But what should we say? What happens when we find ourselves staring silently at the ceiling, wondering if our words are bouncing off of it? Or when we lose our train of thought, what should we do?

Scripture answers these questions with different types of personal prayers. We can use these to prompt our prayers and keep us focused in our time with the Lord.

Adore: Our time with the Lord should always begin with praise. These prayers focus on the character and attributes of God. We celebrate him for who he is and what he has done. The attributes we focus on could be related to specific circumstances in our lives (such as God as our provider or comforter), although our praise should not be dependent on our circumstances (Job 1:21). Or we could praise him for an attribute we are learning more about (such as his sovereignty) during personal Bible study. Praise could also be prompted by specific Bible verses, a situation in the world, or his list of names in Scripture. Whatever attributes we praise him for, our personal prayer time should begin by rejoicing in the truth about God as we approach his throne.

"Through [Jesus] let us continually offer up to God a sacrifice of praise, that is, the fruit of lips that confess his name" (Heb 13:15).

Ask: As we acknowledge who he is and yield to his lordship in our lives, we can then offer prayers for others (intercessions) and prayers for ourselves (petitions). Jesus encouraged us to "ask, and it will be given to you" (Matt 7:7) and assured us, "Whatever you ask in my name, I will do it so that the Father may be glorified in the Son. If you ask me anything in my name, I will do it" (John 14:13–14). These promises affirm his perfect love for us, his perfect plan for us, and his perfect timing for us. Too many times we do not have, because we simply do not ask. And when we do ask, we make our requests with selfish motives (Jas 4:2–3). But if we humbly submit ourselves to God's will, trust him to know and meet our needs, and believe that he will work for our good and his glory, then we can appeal to him in faith and with confidence.

"If you then, who are evil, know how to give good gifts to your children, how much more will your Father in heaven give good things to those who ask him" (Matt 7:11).

Admit: When we are appealing to God in prayer, our faith that he will answer our prayers is never based on our own worthiness. Our best efforts qualify as "polluted garments" before him (Isa 64:6). But he invites us to come to him and be cleansed (Isa 1:18).

This requires us to confess our sins and acknowledge our unrighteousness. If we fail to deal with unconfessed sin in our lives, our prayers will be hindered (Ps 66:18). Through Christ, our admission of guilt is met with his redeeming grace and forgiveness through his blood (Eph 1:7). Too many times as Christians we assume forgiveness, but apart from our repentance and his restoration we cannot walk in fellowship with him (1 John 1:6–7). But "if we confess our sins, he is faithful and righteous to forgive us our sins and to cleanse us from all unrighteousness" (1 John 1:9).

"Search me, God, and know my heart; test me and know my concerns. See if there is any offensive way in me; lead me in the everlasting way" (Ps 139:23–24).

Appreciate: Jesus once healed ten desperately sick men who immediately went to respond with the proper religious duty, but only one returned to say thanks and "give glory to God" (Luke 17:15). Sadly, many Christians resemble the nine who go through the religious motions but never actually stop to give thanks to God. A thankful heart reflects a humble understanding of God's gracious generosity to us in Christ for eternal life (Eph 1:3) and for our earthly life (Jas 1:17). Gratitude is intended to be the disposition of our hearts that overflow with thanksgiving in everything we do (Col 3:17). Giving thanks to God acknowledges our dependence on him, expresses our gratitude for his grace, and displays faith in him to answer our prayers and meet our needs.

"Give thanks in everything; for this is God's will for you in Christ Jesus" (1 Thess 5:18).

These four types of prayers provide a foundational pattern for us to adopt as a personal prayer strategy. By walking through these categories, we can focus our hearts and direct our thoughts during our times of prayer. By beginning with praise, we celebrate God for who and how he is (*Adore*), rejoicing in his greatness and giving him glory. Based on these truths, and our faith in him, we then can appeal to him on behalf of others and call on him to meet our needs (*Ask*). However, we don't presume his goodness to us. In fact, through confession and repentance, we acknowledge our unworthiness, receive his mercy, and renew our faith in Christ (*Admit*). As a result, we can offer our gratitude as we thank him for all that he has done and trust him for all that he will do (*Appreciate*). This strategy and sequence will help us to guard the motives of our hearts, offer prayers in submission to his will, and keep us mindful of his undeserved kindness as we abide in him.

Step 2: Follow a Prayer Schedule. Everybody intends to pray more, but somehow we all find ourselves procrastinating. Sometimes we rationalize it, saying we don't have time, but this is a matter of priorities. Other times we spiritualize it, saying that God knows our needs and hears our hearts. Although Jesus did say that our "Father knows the things you need before you ask him," his very next words were, "Therefore, you should pray" (Matt 6:8–9).

Some Christians resist a prayer schedule, feeling that it removes the spontaneity, and maybe the spirituality, from their prayer life. But being organized does not necessarily quench the Spirit. Setting a schedule protects our time with God, allows us to devote ourselves more fully to him without distractions, and prioritizes our prayer time by planning our days around it. It allows us practically to live out the truth of Matt 6:33, "Seek first the kingdom of God and his righteousness." And it tells God, "You are my first priority. You matter more than anyone or anything."

A scheduled time of prayer also does not eliminate our need to maintain a disposition of heartfelt prayer. Scripture teaches us that we should sustain an ongoing conversation with God throughout the day as we "pray constantly" (1 Thess 5:17). But a designated time of prayer provides the basis for our continued conversation. An in-depth prayer time is the reservoir that supplies one's prayer life throughout the day. Isolated times of prayer allow the moment-by-moment conversations with the Lord to be more personal and natural.

But a prayer schedule involves more than designating a daily time for prayer. It helps us to focus our prayers and maximize our prayer time. Many people struggle to maintain consistency in their prayer lives; when one begins praying for everyone and everything, one's prayer time can extend exponentially. This is where a weekly prayer schedule can be helpful. Although there are some things we should pray for each day, others can be prayed for in an ongoing weekly rotation. A sample schedule could look something like this:

Sunday: Pray for churches—their pastors, their people, their ministries, their services, their outreach, and their unity.

Monday: Pray for family members—immediate and extended family, personal issues, general care, specific needs, and present circumstances (your immediate family is usually included in your daily prayers).

Tuesday: Pray for friends—close friends, distant friends, acquaintances, your personal relationships, strained relationships, gratitude for meaningful relationships, neighbors, coworkers, and for your friends' various life circumstances.

Wednesday: Pray for the lost and missions—lost people in your life, in your community, and around the world; for missionaries and their work; for your evangelistic opportunities, boldness and courage to share, and open hearts that are receptive to the gospel.

Thursday: Pray for leaders—church and denominational leaders, community leaders (school teachers, civil servants, etc.), governmental leaders (national and local); leaders in your workplace, in your church administration, and in your church ministries.

Friday: Pray for your personal needs—struggles, doubts, worries, fears; ambitions, hopes, future direction; finances, health, wisdom, spiritual growth, and ministry opportunities; also include prayers of thanksgiving and praise.

Saturday: Pray with an open heart—prompt your prayers with Scripture; spend time listening to the Lord through reflection and repentance; consider immediate circumstances and focus on yielding to the Spirit's voice and guidance.

These daily emphases are not meant to limit your prayers but are meant to be a guide. You can develop a prayer journal that lists specific names associated with these days, and you can watch God answer your prayers as you record them. Obviously, there will still be time set aside each day for the previously discussed prayer strategy, but these focused prayers will guide your time of supplication and intercession on behalf of others.

Making efficient use of our prayer time, with designated *times* for prayer and specified *types* of prayer, can enhance our prayers' fervency and frequency. In doing so, we can fulfill God's challenge for us, "Pray at all times in the Spirit with every prayer and request, and stay alert with all perseverance and intercession for all the saints" (Eph 6:18).

Prayer is a nonnegotiable in the Christian life. It is a necessity that sustains us and empowers us to overcome the world. Apart from a life bathed in prayer, we will lose heart. Therefore, we should seek God with desperate prayer in a way that acknowledges our complete dependence on him and our hopeless futility apart from him. Through our passionate and persistent appeals to God, we demonstrate a desperate and dependent faith in him. As a result, he will use our prayers to transform our hearts to zealously follow and fulfill his will.

CHAPTER 6

We Must Apply His Truth

We live in a *YAHOO* culture: You Always Have Other Options. The mind-set of preference and unlimited selection permeates everything. Consider a common scenario of sitting down to eat at a restaurant. Your server will approach you to take your drink order. Suppose you ask for tea, you will then be asked to specify, hot tea or iced tea, sweet or unsweet, lemon or no lemon. When someone returns to take your order, you select chicken. You then are presented with a variety of choices: would you like your chicken fried, baked, grilled, Cajun, or as a sandwich? To keep it simple, you choose grilled. The server then asks what you would like for a side. You ask for a potato and are immediately presented with a smorgasbord of potato options: baked, stuffed, sweet, mashed, or fried. Believing that mashed potatoes will be the simplest, you express your desire. Just when you think you've completed the menu labyrinth, your server clarifies, white or brown gravy?

This seemingly absurd, yet everyday example demonstrates the nature of what we are conditioned to expect. The seemingly never-ending combinations of options extends well beyond our meals as almost everything can be tailor-made and suited to your preference. But when it comes to our spiritual growth, there are not unlimited options. Scripture is God's gracious gift and designated means by which we mature. There is no substitute for our source of spiritual nourishment; it's the Bible. If we are going to fulfill God's will, we will accomplish it by the power of God's Word.

Our Recipe for Success

Throughout the Scriptures, God clearly identifies his Word as the primary ingredient to determine our spiritual success. In Josh 1:8, as the mantle of leadership is being passed from Moses to Joshua, God states, "This *book of instruction* must not depart from your mouth; you are to *meditate* on it *day and night* so that you may carefully observe everything written in it. For then you will *prosper* and *succeed* in whatever you do" (italics mine, here and below).

Similarly, the psalmist prescribed the same spiritual recipe for godly success. He describes the necessary devotion of the blessed man, asserting, "his delight is in the LORD*'s instruction*, and he *meditates* on it *day and night*. He is like a tree planted beside flowing streams that bears its fruit in its season and whose leaf does not wither. Whatever he does *prospers*" (Ps 1:2–3). The ingredients almost completely mirror one another with the fundamental element clearly identified as God's Word.

In the New Testament, God commends the same formula. James tells us, "But the one who *looks intently* into the *perfect law* of freedom and *perseveres in it*, and is not a forgetful hearer but a doer who works—this person will be *blessed* in what he does" (Jas 1:25). Again we see, tireless devotion and faithful submission to God's Word yields the spiritual fruit and progress God desires for us. In all three of these passages, it is clear: spiritual growth and success is predicated on Scripture. But why? What unique qualities does Scripture possess that makes Scripture the key ingredient that cannot be replaced?

First, *Scripture records the works of God.* His deeds throughout history, from the miraculous to the typical, are recorded in the Bible. Beginning with the creation of the universe, to the flood, the plagues of Egypt and the parting of the Red Sea, the defeat of his enemies, fulfilled prophecies and promises, to the sacrifice of his own Son for our sins—the list of his mighty works is endless. But these events are not simply recorded for their historical reference. As Paul noted, "Whatever was written in the past was written for our instruction, so that we may have hope through endurance and through the encouragement from the Scriptures" (Rom 15:4). In other words, the Bible records the works of God to teach us what God is capable of and the extent to which he will go on our behalf. These truths are meant to teach us and encourage us.

Second, *Scripture recounts the ways of God.* The Bible does not record God's works as merely factual history; they are explained with divine commentary. Scripture provides insight into how and why God does the things he does. We are not left to wonder as to God's motives, his means, or his agenda. Although we readily affirm God's declaration that his ways are infinitely beyond our ways (Isa 55:8–9), we sometimes fail to recognize that the Lord immediately follows this by clarifying, "For just as rain and snow fall from heaven and do not return there without saturating the earth and making it germinate and sprout, and providing seed to sow and food to eat, so my word that comes from my mouth will not return to me empty, but it will accomplish what I please and will prosper in what I send it to do" (vv. 10–11). God's ways are certainly not our ways, but through his word, he discloses his ways to us and informs our understanding. Therefore, we know that he works through his people; he works through prayer; and he works through our circumstances. These ways, among many others recounted in Scripture, help us to determine how we should live accordingly.

Next, *Scripture reflects the will of God*. Not only does the Bible tell us what God does and how he does it, but it also expresses what he desires. We recognized in an earlier chapter that Scripture explicitly asserts several facets of God's will. In addition, through his works and his ways, we can discern his affections, his desires, and his intentions. These truths help us to determine his will for our lives. As a result, Paul challenges believers to renew their minds and transform their understanding with God's Word, "so that you may discern what is the good, pleasing, and perfect will of God" (Rom 12:2). God's will is clearly reflected in his Word. If we desire to find it, follow it, and fulfill it, his Word will serve as the map to guide us along the way.

Finally, and perhaps most important, *Scripture reveals the "who" of God*. As finite beings, it is impossible for us to conceive of an infinite and transcendent God. Therefore, it was necessary for God to accommodate himself to us by divine self-disclosure. When we read God's Word, he is revealing himself to us. Every page and passage teaches us something about who and how he is. This should be our primary goal whenever we come to God's Word, to know him more fully.

These attributes of Scripture highlight its unique nature and clearly establish it as the key ingredient in God's recipe for success. Therefore, we must devote ourselves to becoming faithful students of his Word and allow it to permeate all aspects of our lives.

Our Reliance on Scripture

Our success in every area of life will be determined by our reliance on God's Word. Scripture provides everything we need to succeed for Christ when we allow it to inform and infuse our lives. As we evaluate several specific arenas of life, we can consider the role of Scripture in the success of each one.

Success in our worship. Our worship includes more than singing songs at our corporate gatherings. It is a lifestyle, a disposition of the heart, that submits every area of our lives to the praise and glory of God (1 Cor 10:31). True worship surrenders our lives as "a living sacrifice, holy and pleasing to God," in a way that ascribes worth and honor to the lordship of Christ (Rom 12:1).

As we noted, Scripture teaches us God's will and his ways, what he desires and what he does. Therefore, when we align our lives with his Word, we can know that we are honoring him. By allowing Scripture to inform and infuse our lives, our lifestyles of worship will be pleasing and acceptable to God.

Although a lifestyle of worship includes more than our corporate praise, it is also epitomized by our collective celebrations as his people. We see the role of Scripture in this aspect of worship as well. The Bible instructs us, "Let the word of Christ dwell richly among you, in all wisdom teaching and admonishing one another through psalms, hymns, and spiritual songs, singing to God with gratitude in your hearts" (Col 3:16). God's Word must saturate our songs. With Scripture as the substance of what we affirm and voice in praise to God, our corporate worship will be used by him to counsel, instruct, and transform our lives.

Success in our walk. Our relationship with the Lord is often described as our walk. The Bible characterizes the personal and ongoing fellowship God has with his people in this way (Gen 6:9). More specifically, it describes our everyday behavior as we journey through life and maintain a close relationship with Jesus. As the Bible instructs us, "The one who says he remains in him should walk just as he walked" (1 John 2:6). Success in our daily walk with Christ will certainly depend on our reliance on Scripture.

Success in our walk primarily involves our spiritual growth. Jesus affirmed that our spiritual progress, or sanctification, would be accomplished by God's Word (John 17:17). This is why Peter challenged believers, "Like newborn infants, desire the pure milk of the word, so that you may grow up into your salvation" (1 Pet 2:2). Paul instructed Timothy that all Scripture is beneficial for teaching, training, and growing us so that we are fully equipped to fulfill God's will for our lives (2 Tim 3:16–17).

Success in our walk also includes our victory over temptation and sin. We are told that Scripture is God's scalpel for performing spiritual surgery on our hearts, dissecting its thoughts and motives, and cutting out those areas infected by sin (Heb 4:12). At the same time, it is a weapon for battle, the "sword of the Spirit," that equips us to stand firm and resist the spiritual enemies that attack us (Eph 6:10–17). Jesus wielded God's Word and defeated Satan's attacks when the enemy tempted him in the wilderness (Matt 4:1–11). The psalmist affirmed that our way will be kept pure when we keep it according to God's Word (Ps 119:9). Therefore, he determined, "I have treasured your word in my heart so that I may not sin against you" (v. 11). Our walk with the Lord will be successful when we inform and infuse it with Scripture.

Success in our work. Oftentimes we divorce our spiritual lives from our daily lives. We are guilty of separating our work from our walk. But God doesn't make that same distinction. Our work, whether that's at a place of employment, at a school, or in the church, is part of God's will for our lives that requires our reliance on his Word.

Scripture teaches us that our work, and whatever achievements come from it, cannot be viewed as that which is performed by our determination or our efforts. God reminded Israel that even their ability to perform work came from him, and, as a result, they must acknowledge and appreciate his hand in all that is accomplished (Deut 8:17–19). The Christian life is often characterized by comfort, but in reality it is depicted as one of sacrifice and struggle. For example, Paul's commendation of the Thessalonians seems to drip with beads of sweat on the page as he affirms, "your *work* produced by faith, your *labor* motivated by love, and your *endurance* inspired by hope" (1 Thess 1:3).

From a practical standpoint, our work serves as a primary avenue for our testimony for Christ. As Paul noted, you should "seek to lead a quiet life, to mind your own business, and to work with your own hands, as we commanded you, so that you may behave properly in the presence of outsiders and not be dependent on anyone" (1 Thess 4:11–12). Sadly, too many times, Christian employees are known for being late, lazy, or lackadaisical. But it ought to be the opposite. Believers should be the ones who are known as the most committed, hardest-working, and responsible employees. We must adopt the biblical mentality, "Whatever you do, do it from the heart, as something done for the Lord and not for people" (Col 3:23). When our work ethic and efforts are informed and infused by Scripture, we will be successful in our service for Christ.

Success in our witness. The source of salvation is the truth of the gospel (Rom 1:16). But our understanding of the good news of Jesus Christ comes from its revelation through the Scriptures (2 Tim 3:15). Salvation through faith in Jesus's substitutionary death on the cross for our sins requires a fundamental understanding of God's holiness, humanity's sinfulness, and Christ's forgiveness. These foundational truths are all revealed in the Word of God.

Scripture also informs us of God's divine mandate for those who have been transformed by the good news to share the good news (Matt 28:18–20). We have the privilege, and the obligation, to participate in God's redemptive plan by reaching the lost with the gospel. This requires us to make the most of every opportunity as we engage our world for Christ by knowing how to respond to each person (Col 4:5–6). When we inform and infuse our witness with Scripture, we will always be prepared "to give a defense to anyone who asks you for a reason for the hope that is in you" (1 Pet 3:15).

Although these four life arenas are not comprehensive, through them we can recognize the foundational nature of the Scriptures for success in every area of our lives. For God's Word to permeate your heart and life, it requires a calculated effort and strategy.

Living It Out

Affirming the significance of Scripture without establishing a strategy to implement it is pointless. We must now consider the steps that are necessary to rely on Scripture as the foundational truth and fundamental ingredient for success in every area of our lives.

Step 1: Submerge Yourself in Scripture. For God's Word to permeate our lives, we must immerse our hearts in Scripture. Sadly, most Christians have very limited exposure to the Bible, not because their access is restricted, but because they forfeit the opportunity. Most people are content to absorb biblical truth by listening to Christian radio, listening to an occasional podcast, reading a Christian's blog post, or sitting through a weekly sermon. Although all of these are helpful supplements to a spiritual diet, there must be a steady intake of God's Word for us to become spiritually healthy and strong. There are several ways for us to submerge ourselves in Scripture.

First, we must *read God's Word daily.* Nobody sits down to eat once a week. Yet many Christians expect to be nourished and satisfied by weekly Bible studies or sermons. Jesus explained that both physical and spiritual nourishment are essential, and Scripture is the source of sustenance for our soul. "Man must not live on bread alone but on every word that comes from the mouth of God" (Matt 4:4). As Jesus taught us to pray, every physical aspect of his model prayer has a spiritual parallel. This means that our prayer, "Give us today our daily bread" (Matt 6:11), involves relying on God to provide for our basic needs, but also includes coming to his Word for our daily nourishment.

The most effective way to maintain consistency in daily Scripture intake is to follow a Bible reading plan. A variety of available options feature different amounts of biblical intake each day and operate on different schedules, but the goal for each of us must be consistent exposure to the "living and effective" Word of God (Heb 4:12). Daily Bible reading is not intended to be in-depth, prolonged Bible study. This is designed to be an intentional effort to read God's Word, to hear him speak, and to learn to love the Scriptures.

If we are honest, there are days when we read God's Word and don't feel as if we're getting anything out of it. But emotions cannot determine our commitment. If you've ever been outside for an extended period of time on a cloudy day, you may not "feel" as if you are getting sunburned. But when you step into a warm shower, the tingling sensation on the back of your neck might confirm the sunlight's effects. The same is true for reading Scripture. Even when we do not feel as if it is having an effect, our exposure to its radiating power always has an impact on us. Therefore, daily Bible reading is a necessity.

Second, we must also *read God's Word devotionally.* Devotional Bible reading typically has a guide that includes a specific verse or passage each day with some explanatory thoughts and practical application. Some Christians want to believe that they've outgrown devotionals. But a refusal to benefit from them is simply prideful. Devotionals are helpful because they provide a particular verse or biblical thought that can be prayed over and thought about throughout the day. Although you may be able to identify a verse from your daily Bible reading, you will often find yourself "looking" for that verse rather than simply soaking in the Scriptures. The goal with a devotional is to apply a biblical truth to your life each day.

Your devotional can be read at the same time or at a different time altogether from your daily reading. Like Bible reading plans, these come in a variety of formats. One of the most important factors in selecting a devotional is to choose a trusted author who is theologically and biblically sound. You also should look for a devotional that doesn't completely isolate a verse from its context but rather explains the verse according to the broader purpose of its passage. When you read the Scriptures devotionally, like the psalmist you can pray, "Help me understand your instruction, and I will obey it and follow it with all my heart" (Ps 119:34).

Third, we must *read God's Word deeply.* Our knowledge of God's Word cannot remain customary and familiar. We must be willing to dig deep to build our lives on the sure foundation of the divine truth (Luke 6:47–48). We must become diligent students of God's Word, who handle it correctly and have no reason to be ashamed (2 Tim 2:15). Too many times, Christians remain shallow in their understanding when God wants us all to grow in our knowledge of him through his Word. God challenges us to grow, recognizing our propensity to be spiritually complacent.

Although by this time you ought to be teachers, you need someone to teach you the basic principles of God's revelation again. You need milk, not solid food. Now everyone who lives on milk is inexperienced with the message about righteousness, because he is an infant. But solid food is for the mature—for those whose senses have been trained to distinguish between good and evil. (Heb 5:12–14)

Deeper Bible study requires greater amounts of time and effort. Many Christians make the mistake of trying to accomplish in one devotional reading what should be extended over several days or even weeks. In-depth study does not necessarily follow a specific timeline. It can explore a specific topic, a particular passage, or a biblical book as you are able to spend time diving into God's Word. It can be part of an ongoing study, a follow up to a sermon, or the homework for a discipleship group. When you attempt to study the Bible deeply on a daily basis, you will more than likely grow frustrated as you frequently fall behind or find yourself rushing just to complete study material that day. We must make studying God's Word a priority while also making sure that we are spending the time necessary to absorb the information and listen to God's voice. Studying God's Word deeply is an ongoing and lifelong journey that will enrich our lives in every way. When combined with daily and devotional study of the Scriptures, we will be fully submerged in the life-changing truth of the Bible.

Step 2: Saturate Yourself with Scripture. As we submerge ourselves in God's Word, we must also soak it in and allow it to saturate our hearts. A rock can be submerged in water but not absorb it. By contrast, a sponge soaks it in, so that even when it is pulled out of the water it is still gushing from within.

To saturate ourselves with God's Word *we must meditate on Scripture*. At the beginning of this chapter, we recognized that the recipe for success included consistently dwelling on God's Word. Joshua was instructed to "meditate on it day and night" (Josh 1:8). The psalmist informed us that God's blessing rested on the one who delights in God's Word and "meditates on it day and night" (Ps 1:2).

This involves allowing Scripture to become the backdrop for your thoughts, the screen saver for your mind, and the focus of your daydreams. It is an intentional effort to concentrate on the truth of God's Word and to evaluate all of life through the lens of Scripture.

When we meditate on Scripture, we allow it to dictate our thoughts, saturate our hearts, and permeate our lives. Just like preparing a savory meal for the grill, we often marinate the entrée and allow it to soak in all the flavors of our favorite sauces. Similarly, we must marinate our hearts with God's Word, soaking it in, and allowing its satisfying goodness to nourish our souls. We meditate on Scripture when we voice God's Word as the substance of our prayers. We also meditate on it when we contemplate its meaning, submit to its authority, and consider how to apply it to our lives.

Saturating ourselves with God's Word also means that *we memorize Scripture*. Sometimes we commit verses to memory as a result of carefully meditating on them. However, most of the time memorization requires study and repetition. You may be reading this, thinking, "That sounds good, but I stink at memorizing. I can't remember anything." Yet when prompted, you can recite your address, your phone number, your birthdate, your passwords for multiple sites, and countless other practical facts. You also can sing the lyrics to your favorite songs without strain or maybe quote inane sports statistics. You may object, "That's not the same thing. I use those things every day." My point exactly! Anyone can memorize, it just requires regular effort and commitment.

Many people see memorizing Scripture as reserved for the spiritually elite or the intellectually gifted. But committing God's Word to memory is really just allowing Scripture to implant within your heart (Jas 1:21). We have recognized the personal benefits as we observed the success that results when our worship, our walk, our work, and our witness are informed and infused with Scripture. This becomes possible when we memorize God's Word, and the Spirit can bring it to mind at the appropriate time or point of need.

We also can recognize how committed verses of Scripture can equip us for ministering to others. An encouraging note in a card or text, a word of advice or personal counsel, a prayer shared during a difficult time, a thoughtful response to a doctrinal question or cultural situation, or cross references when preparing or teaching a Bible study—all are practical ways your ministry to others will be enhanced by memorizing Scripture.

Practically speaking, memorizing Scripture must be approached with pure motives and a realistic strategy. The goal is not to impress people; it is to impact people. The power of God's Word can penetrate hearts and change lives. To memorize Scripture effectively, we must be steady and consistent. For example, a verse a week is not mentally taxing or overly impressive, but, over the period of four years, there is the potential of more than two hundred verses committed to heart. You would be a walking Bible!

Scripture is also best memorized in context and with content. Knowing where a verse is located and the context around it helps the Scripture attach to our understanding and more readily "stick." Therefore, we should memorize the reference, or address, of the verse. This will also allow you to point others to the verses as you minister. In memorizing Scripture, it is also helpful for the content of the verses selected to be relevant and applicable. If you are struggling with worry or lust, choose verses on those topics. If you are going through a difficult time, study Scriptures on trials, faith, and hope. If you are focused on a specific topic or doctrinal truth, commit to memory verses related to your subject and passions. All of these tips can help you faithfully memorize Scripture and saturate your heart with God's Word.

Step 3: Submit Yourself to Scripture. Knowledge without application is empty and fruitless. To be transformed by God's Word, the most important step is our submission to its authority in our lives through our obedience to it. Submitting ourselves to Scripture requires us to consider how we regard the Bible and, as a result, how we respond to the Bible.

First, we must *treasure God's Word because it's valuable.* Our submission to Scripture is directly related to how we view it. The Bible is God's divine self-disclosure, revealing himself to us (2 Tim 3:16). As such, it is perfect and without error, or "inerrant." We also recognize that it is "inspired." It is God talking to us personally as he speaks through what he has spoken to the prophets and by the human authors (Heb 1:1; 2 Pet 1:20–21). And although it is God's direct message to us, many Christians leave it in their car, on their nightstand, or on a shelf throughout the week and pick it up only to carry it to church.

But when we recognize it as God's Word, we must learn to treasure it. Though it is not our most expensive possession, it should be our most valued earthly possession. The psalmist understood this and declared the Scriptures to be "more desirable than gold—than an abundance of pure gold" (Ps 19:10). When we recognize its incredible worth, we will consume his Word and it will become the delight and joy of our hearts (Jer 15:16). We should be willing to gladly submit our lives to his immeasurably valuable divine revelation.

Submission to Scripture also means that we should *trust God's Word because it's reliable.* The Bible guides us and instructs us as we navigate through life (Ps 119:105). Because it is inerrant and inspired, we can also have confidence that it will not mislead us in any way. This means that it is "infallible." But it is not just a book of suggestions. As God's Word, it deserves and demands our obedience. The promises it contains, the assurances it offers, and the trustworthy counsel it provides are all accessed and experienced through our submission to it.

The verses in the recipe for success confirm this. Joshua was instructed to meditate on God's Word, so that he could "carefully observe everything written in it" (Josh 1:8). James instructed believers that obedience must complement their hearing and understanding, not as "a forgetful hearer but a doer who works" (Jas 1:25). Likewise, Jesus taught that it was the one who hears his words and "acts on them" who establishes life on the sure foundation of his word (Matt 7:24–27). If we want to know about God, we can know the Bible, but if we want to know God, we must obey the Bible!

If we follow God's recipe for success, we will recognize the need to rely on Scripture in every area of our lives. This requires a response and strategy that helps us to become lifelong students of God's Word. When we submerge ourselves in Scripture, saturate ourselves with Scripture, and submit ourselves to Scripture, God will use his divine truth to conform us to the likeness of Jesus and guide us as we find, follow, and fulfill his will for our lives.

Concluding Thoughts

So what does all of this mean? As you discern and pursue God's will for you, where will this journey lead? What exactly is God's plan for your life? Although the specifics are personally unique for each one of us and should be explored through the principles we've covered, there are some final guiding precepts that can help you in your daily walk as you find, follow, and fulfill God's will for your life. They are summed up in this practical and profound verse found in Paul's letter to the Colossians.

Colossians 3:23: Whatever you do, do it from the heart, as something done for the Lord and not for people.

What You Do Matters

The initial phrase in this verse, "Whatever you do," is a comprehensive expression that means God has expectations for anything and everything that we do. *What* we do matters to him. From our life-changing decisions—choice of college, career path, whom we marry, where we live—to our everyday choices, none of them is insignificant. The details of our lives, big and small, are important to God because he cares about us. Therefore, "*whatever* you do"—the friends you associate with, the places you go, how you spend your free time—must be considered and chosen based on what Scripture says will honor Christ. In this sense, his desires for all of our lives share a common principle that is not personally specific. *Whatever* we do must please and honor the Lord.

At the same time, your calling is unique. Your giftedness, your life's passions, your personality, and your skills—all blend together to form a personal calling and journey that is different from anyone else's. Although others may have the same career with similar abilities and a kindred spirit, God's will for you is specifically designed for you. Therefore, "whatever *you* do" has expectations associated with his personal plan for your life. You have been set apart to serve a particular purpose in his kingdom. This means that you can live with confidence and assurance that your life has value and significance. It cannot be measured by salary, status, prominence, or prestige. Your calling, regardless of how the world appraises it, is a divine privilege with eternal worth. What you do matters to God.

How You Do It Matters

Not only is *what* we do significant to God, but *how* we do it matters to him as well. We all know what it is like to witness (or be!) a teenager who complies with a parent's requests to do a household chore only to grumble and complain the whole time. Or to see a student who easily does enough to pass but clearly doesn't do his or her best. This verse tells us that whatever we do for the Lord, we must "do it from the heart." Disgruntled attitudes, halfhearted attempts, or dishonorable approaches in accomplishing God's will ultimately nullify whatever obedience we believe we've achieved.

This simple phrase, "from the heart," speaks to our effort and our excellence. A sincere effort will go all out, motivate you to work your hardest and persevere when things get hard. It will not take advantage of others by dumping responsibilities on them or unjustly benefiting from their work. It will not abuse opportunities by taking shortcuts or misusing privileges. Effort that honors the Lord will operate with integrity. "From the heart" also describes the quality of our work. What you do for the Lord should be done with excellence, doing your best to honor him. He is worthy of whatever sacrifice this may require. We should adopt the heart of King David when he declared, "I will not offer to the LORD my God . . . offerings that cost me nothing" (2 Sam 24:24). *What* you do for the Lord matters, but it's not the only thing that does. *How* you do it matters just as much.

Why You Do It Matters

What ultimately determines our consistency and faithfulness to our calling will not be how much we enjoy it, how successful we become, or how smoothly things go. Longevity in the Christian walk, especially in our dedication to our calling, will ultimately be determined by the source of our motivation. The final phrase of this verse, "as something done for the Lord and not for people" drills down beneath the surface to reveal the heart beneath our actions. This means it's not just *what* we do, and *how* we do it, but *why* we do it that matters.

Many people, including believers, can be motivated by selfish and impure desires. Some incentives, such as material wealth, personal pleasure, or notoriety, are blatantly sinful and obvious. Others can be masked by honorable or spiritual intentions. Christians can be deceived by their own hearts into believing they are serving the Lord for the sake of their families, to help others, or because they feel indebted to the Lord. These are certainly noble ambitions, but many times they become spiritualized alibis that mask true motives. We must be careful to see our hearts the way God sees them.

113

Scripture cautions, "All a person's ways seem right to him, but the LORD weighs motives" (Prov 16:2).

Sadly, in the pursuit of their callings, many Christians are not misguided by their own hearts but by well-intending loved ones, mentors, or friends. Sometimes teachers, pastors, friends, and parents can exert influence on a willing and vulnerable person to pursue a career that is ultimately not part of God's plan for them. Other times, these leaders may rightly recognize the Lord's call on a person's life, but their ill-timed or overbearing pressure may lead to resistance or resentment.

But this phrase, "as something done for the Lord and not for people," liberates all of us from pressure we put on ourselves or others place on us. It relieves the tension we can feel from competing interests. It can gauge our motives and, when necessary, help us to recalibrate. Ultimately it serves as the inexhaustible fuel that strengthens us to persevere; it sustains us through emotionally and circumstantially difficult seasons. When motivated by your love for the Lord and your passion for his glory, you can live with joy, freedom, and gratitude. As you find, follow, and fulfill his will for your life, remember, "Whatever you do, in word or in deed, do everything in the name of the Lord Jesus, giving thanks to God the Father through him" (Col 3:17).

Subject Index

Scripture Index